THE TRUTH ABOUT
_____

grace

THE TRUTH ABOUT

grace

John MacArthur

THOMAS NELSON
Since 1798

NASHVILLE   DALLAS   MEXICO CITY   RIO DE JANEIRO

Published in Nashville, Tennessee, by Thomas Nelson. Thomas Nelson is a registered trademark of Thomas Nelson, Inc.

Thomas Nelson, Inc., titles may be purchased in bulk for educational, business, fund-raising, or sales promotional use. For information, please e-mail SpecialMarkets@ThomasNelson.com.

Unleashing God's Truth, One Verse at a Time® is a trademark of Grace to You. All rights reserved.

Compiled from previously published material in *The God Who Loves*, *The Jesus You Can't Ignore*, *The Vanishing Conscience*, *Hard to Believe*, *The Truth War*, and *The Gospel According to the Apostles*.

Unless otherwise indicated, Scripture quotations are taken from THE NEW KING JAMES VERSION. © 1982 by Thomas Nelson, Inc. Used by permission. All rights reserved.

Scripture quotations marked NIV are taken from the Holy Bible, New International Version®, NIV®. Copyright © 1973, 1978, 1984 by Biblica, Inc.™ Used by permission of Zondervan. All rights reserved worldwide. www.zondervan.com

Scripture quotations marked NASB are taken from the NEW AMERICAN STANDARD BIBLE®. © The Lockman Foundation 1960, 1962, 1963, 1968, 1971, 1972, 1973, 1975, 1977, 1995. Used by permission.

Scripture quotations marked KJV are taken from the King James Version.

Library of Congress Cataloging-in-Publication Data

MacArthur, John, 1939-
  The truth about grace / John MacArthur.
    p. cm.
  Includes bibliographical references (p.   ).
  ISBN 978-1-4002-0412-0
1. Grace (Theology) I. Title.
  BT761.3.M27 2012
  234—dc23

Printed in the United States of America

12 13 14 15 16 QG 6 5 4 3 2 1

CONTENTS

CHAPTER 1

GRACE DEFINED

WHAT IS GRACE?

Defining *grace* succinctly is notoriously difficult. Some of the most detailed theology textbooks do not offer any concise definition of the term. Someone has proposed an acronym: GRACE is *God's Riches At Christ's Expense*. That's not a bad way to characterize grace, but it is not a sufficient theological definition. One of the best-known definitions of grace is only three words: *God's unmerited favor*. A. W. Tozer expanded on that: "Grace is the good pleasure of God that inclines him to bestow benefits on the undeserving."[1] Louis Berkhof is more to the point: grace is "the unmerited operation of God in the heart of man, effected through the agency of the Holy Spirit."[2]

At the heart of the term *grace* is the idea of divine favor. The Hebrew word for grace is *cheμn*, used, for example, in Genesis 6:8: "Noah found favor in the eyes of the LORD" (NASB). Closely related is the verb *chaμnan*, meaning "to show favor." In the New Testament, *grace* is a rendering of the Greek *charis*, meaning "gracefulness," "graciousness," "favor," or "gratitude." Intrinsic to its meaning are the ideas of favor, goodness, and goodwill.

Grace is all that and more. Grace is not merely unmerited favor; it is favor bestowed on sinners who deserve wrath. Showing kindness to a stranger is "unmerited favor"; doing good to one's enemies is more the spirit of grace (Luke 6:27–36). Grace is not a dormant or abstract quality, but a dynamic, active, working principle: "The grace of God has appeared, bringing salvation . . . and instructing us" (Titus 2:11–12 NASB). It is not some kind of ethereal blessing that lies idle until we appropriate it. Grace is God's sovereign initiative to sinners (Ephesians 1:5–6). Grace is not a one-time event in the Christian experience. We stand in grace (Romans 5:2). The entire Christian life is driven and empowered by grace: "It is good for the heart to be strengthened by grace, not by foods" (Hebrews 13:9 NASB). Peter said we should "grow in the grace and knowledge of our Lord and Savior Jesus Christ" (2 Peter 3:18).

Thus we could properly define *grace* as "the free and benevolent influence of a holy God operating sovereignly in the lives of undeserving sinners."

Graciousness is an attribute of God. It is His nature to bestow grace. "He is gracious and compassionate and righteous" (Psalm 112:4 NASB). "He is gracious and compassionate, slow to anger, abounding in loving-kindness, and relenting of evil" (Joel 2:13 NASB). He is "the God of all grace" (1 Peter 5:10); His Son is "full of grace and truth" (John 1:14); His Spirit is "the Spirit of grace" (Hebrews 10:29). Berkhof observed, "While we sometimes speak of grace as an inherent quality, it is in reality the active communication of divine blessings by the inworking of the Holy Spirit, out of the fullness of Him who is 'full of grace and truth.'"[3]

Charis is found in the Greek text 155 times, 100 times in the Pauline epistles alone. Interestingly, the term itself is never used in reference to divine grace in any of the recorded words of Jesus. But grace permeated all His ministry and teaching ("The blind receive sight and the lame walk, the lepers are cleansed and the deaf hear, and the dead are raised up, and the poor have the gospel preached to them" [Matthew 11:5 NASB]; "Come to Me, all who are weary and heavy-laden, and I will give you rest" [Matthew 11:28 NASB]). Grace is a gift.[4] God "gives more grace. . . . [He] gives grace to the humble" (James 4:6). "Of His fullness we have all received, and grace for grace" (John 1:16). Christians are said to be "stewards of the manifold grace of God" (1 Peter 4:10). But that does not mean that God's grace is placed at our disposal. We do not possess God's grace or control its operation. We are subject to grace, never vice versa.

Paul frequently contrasted grace with law (Romans 4:16; 5:20; 6:14–15; Galatians 2:21; 5:4). He was careful to state, however, that grace does not nullify the moral demands of God's law. Rather, it fulfills the righteousness of the law (Romans 6:14–15). In a sense, grace is to law what miracles are to nature. It rises above and accomplishes what law cannot (Romans 8:3). Yet it does not annul the righteous demands of the law; it confirms and validates them (Romans 3:31). Grace has its own law, a higher, liberating law: the law of the Spirit of life in Christ Jesus has set you free from the law of sin and death (Romans 8:2; James 1:25). Note that this new law emancipates us from *sin* as well as *death*. Paul was explicit about this: "What shall we say then? Are we to continue in sin that grace might increase? May it never be! How shall we who died to sin still live in it?" (Romans 6:1–2 NASB). Grace reigns through *righteousness* (Romans 5:21).

TWO KINDS OF GRACE

Common Grace

Theologians speak of *common grace* and *special grace*.

Common grace is a term theologians use to describe the goodness of God to all mankind universally. Common grace restrains sin and the effects of sin on the human race. Common grace is what keeps humanity from descending into the morass of evil that we would see if the full expression of our fallen nature were allowed to have free reign.

Scripture teaches that we are totally depraved—tainted with sin in every aspect of our being (Romans 3:10–18). People who doubt this doctrine often ask, "How can people who are supposedly totally depraved enjoy beauty, have a sense of right and wrong, know the pangs of a wounded conscience, or produce great works of art and literature? Aren't these accomplishments of humanity proof that the human race is essentially good? Don't these things testify to the basic goodness of human nature?"

And the answer is no. Human nature is utterly corrupt. "There is none righteous, no, not one" (Romans 3:10). "The heart is more deceitful than all else and is desperately sick" (Jeremiah 17:9 NASB). Unregenerate men and women are "dead in trespasses and sins" (Ephesians 2:1). All people are by nature "foolish . . . disobedient, deceived, enslaved to various lusts and pleasures, spending [their lives] in malice" (Titus 3:3 NASB). This is true of all alike, "For all have sinned and fall short of the glory of God" (Romans 3:23).

Common grace is all that restrains the full expression of human sinfulness. God has graciously given us a conscience, which enables us to know the difference between right and wrong, and to some degree places moral constraints on evil behavior (Romans 2:15). He sovereignly maintains order in human society through government (Romans 13:1–5). He enables us to admire beauty and goodness (Psalm 50:2). He imparts numerous advantages, blessings, and tokens of His kindness indiscriminately on both the evil and the good, the righteous and the unrighteous (Matthew 5:45). All of those things are the result of common grace, God's goodness to mankind in general.

Common grace *ought* to be enough to move sinners to repentance. The apostle Paul rebukes the unbeliever: "Do you think lightly of the riches of His kindness and tolerance and patience, not knowing that the kindness of God leads you to repentance?" (Romans 2:4 NASB). Yet because of the depth of depravity in the human heart, all sinners spurn the goodness of God.

Common grace does not pardon sin or redeem sinners, but it is nevertheless a sincere token of God's goodwill to mankind in general. As the apostle Paul said, "In Him we live and move and have our being . . . for we also are His offspring" (Acts 17:28). That takes in everyone on earth, not just those whom God adopts as sons. God deals with us all as His offspring, people made in His image. "The LORD is good to all, and His tender mercies are over all His works" (Psalm 145:9).

If you question the love and goodness of God to all, look again at the world in which we live. Someone might say, "There's a lot of sorrow in this world." The only reason the sorrow and tragedy stand out is because there is also much joy and gladness. The only reason we recognize the ugliness is that God has given us so much beauty. The only reason we feel the disappointment is that there is so much that satisfies.

When we understand that all of humanity is fallen and rebellious and unworthy of any blessing from God's hand, it helps give a better perspective. "Because of the LORD's great love we are not consumed, for his compassions never fail" (Lamentations 3:22 NIV). And the only reason God ever gives us anything to laugh at, smile at, or enjoy is because He is a good and loving God. If He were not, we would be immediately consumed by His wrath.

Acts 14 contains a helpful description of common grace. Here Paul and Barnabas were ministering at Lystra, when Paul healed a lame man. The crowds saw it and someone began saying that Paul was Zeus and Barnabas was Hermes. The priest at the local temple of Zeus wanted to organize a sacrifice to Zeus. But when Paul and Barnabas heard about it, they said,

Men, why are you doing these things? We are also men of the same nature as you, and preach the gospel to you in order that you should turn from these vain things to a living God, who made the heaven and the earth and the sea, and all that is in them. *And in the generations gone by He permitted all the nations to go their own ways; and yet He did not leave Himself without witness, in that*

He did good and gave you rains from heaven and
fruitful seasons, satisfying your hearts with food
and gladness. (vv. 15–17 NASB, emphasis added)

That is a fine description of common grace. While allowing sinners to "go their own ways," God nevertheless bestows on them temporal tokens of His goodness and lovingkindness. It is not saving grace. It has no redemptive effect. Nevertheless, it is a genuine and unfeigned manifestation of divine lovingkindness to all people.

Special Grace

Special grace, better called saving grace, is the irresistible work of God that frees men and women from the penalty and power of sin, renewing the inner person and sanctifying the sinner through the operation of the Holy Spirit. Normally when the New Testament uses the term *grace*, the reference is to saving grace. Throughout this book when I speak of grace, I mean saving grace unless I specify otherwise. Saving grace "reign[s] through righteousness to eternal life" (Romans 5:21).

Grace saves, sanctifies, and brings the soul to glory (Romans 8:29–30). Every stage of the process of salvation is governed by sovereign grace. In fact, the term *grace* in the New Testament is often used as a synonym for the whole of the saving process, particularly in the Pauline epistles (1 Corinthians 1:4; 2 Corinthians 6:1; Galatians 2:21). Paul saw redemption as so utterly a work of God's grace that he often used the word *grace* as a blanket term to refer to the totality of salvation. Grace oversees all of salvation, beginning to end. It never stalls before concluding its work, nor does it ever botch the job.

What we're really saying is that grace is *efficacious*. In other words, grace is certain to produce the intended results. God's grace is *always* efficacious. That truth is rooted in Scripture. It was a major theme of Augustine's teaching. The doctrine of efficacious grace is the bedrock of Reformed *soteriology* (teaching about salvation). Charles Hodge defined efficacious grace as "the almighty power of God."

"No-lordship theology" (denying that salvation and lordship are linked) is fundamentally a denial of efficacious grace. The "grace" described in no-lordship teaching is not certain to accomplish its purposes— and most often, it seems, it does not. Under no-lordship grace, key parts of the process—including repentance, commitment, surrender, and even holiness—are optional aspects of the Christian experience, left up to the believer himself.[5] The believer's faith might even grind to a screeching halt. Yet no-lordship grace tells us we are not supposed to conclude that "he or she was never a believer in the first place."[6] Well then, what are we to conclude? That saving grace is not efficacious?

It is the only reasonable conclusion we can draw from no-lordship theology: "God's miracle of salvation in our lives, accomplished by grace through faith without works, makes ample provision for the lifetime of good works for which he has designed us. But it does not guarantee this."[7]

One could legitimately characterize the whole lordship controversy as a dispute over efficacious grace. All points in the discussion ultimately come back to this: Does God's saving grace inevitably obtain its desired effects? If all sides could come to consensus on that one question, the debate would be settled.

SOVEREIGN GRACE

It is clear from all this that the sovereignty of God in salvation is at the heart of the lordship debate. The irony is that the so-called Grace Movement denies the whole point of grace: that it is God who effects the complete saving work in sinners. Redemption is all His work. God is wholly sovereign in the exercise of His grace; He is not subject to the human will. "For He says to Moses, 'I will have mercy on whom I have mercy, and I will have compassion on whom I have compassion.' So then it does not depend on the man who wills or the man who runs, but on God who has mercy" (Romans 9:15–16 NASB).

Don't misunderstand; we are not idle in the process. Nor does saving grace force people to believe against their will. That is not what irresistible grace means. Grace is not coercion. But by transforming the heart, grace makes the believer wholly willing to trust and obey.

Scripture makes clear that every aspect of grace is God's sovereign work. He foreknows and foreordains the elect (Romans 8:29), calls the sinner to Himself (Romans 8:30), draws the soul to Christ (John 6:44), accomplishes the new birth (John 1:13; James 1:18), grants repentance (Acts 11:18) and faith (Romans 12:3; Acts 18:27), justifies the believer (Romans 3:24; 8:30), makes the redeemed holy (Ephesians 2:10), and finally glorifies him (Romans 8:30).

In no stage of the process is grace thwarted by human failure, dependent on human merit, or subjugated to human effort. "What then shall we say to these things? If God is for us, who can be against us? He who did not spare His own Son, but delivered Him up for us all, how shall He not with Him also freely give us all things?" (Romans 8:30–32). That's grace.

Many people struggle with the concept of sovereign grace, but if God is not sovereign in the exercise of His grace, then it is not grace at all. If God's purposes were dependent on some self-generated response of faith or on human merit, then God Himself would not be sovereign, and salvation would not be wholly

His work. If that were the case, the redeemed would have something to boast about, and grace wouldn't be grace (Romans 3:27; Ephesians 2:9).

Furthermore, because of human depravity, there is nothing in a fallen, reprobate sinner that desires God or is capable of responding in faith. Paul wrote, "There is none who understands, there is none who seeks for God; all have turned aside, together they have become useless; there is none who does good, there is not even one. Their throat is an open grave, with their tongues they keep deceiving, the poison of asps is under their lips" (Romans 3:11–13 NASB). Note the metaphors involving death. That is the state of everyone in sin. As we shall see shortly, Scripture teaches that sinful humanity is dead in trespasses and sins (Ephesians 2:1), "separate[d] from Christ, excluded from the commonwealth of Israel, and strangers to the covenants of promise, having no hope and without God in the world" (v. 12 NASB). There is no escape from such a desperate predicament, except for the sovereign intervention of God's saving grace.

CHAPTER 2

GRACE RECEIVED

GRACE FROM THE KING

Every believer receives the grace of God as a result of responding to the good news. And the good news is that salvation is by grace.

The apostle Paul said, "For by grace you have been saved through faith, and that not of yourselves; it is the gift of God, not of works, lest anyone should boast" (Ephesians 2:8–9). The grace of God that brings salvation has appeared to all people. It is offered totally apart from anything we could ever do to receive God's favor. It is the unmerited favor of God, who in His mercy and lovingkindness grants us salvation as a gift. All we have to do is simply respond by believing in His Son.

We enter the kingdom of God only by the grace of God. There is no place for self-congratulations or human achievement. Remember to thank God for granting you such a gracious salvation.

UNDESERVED FAVOR

Salvation does not come by confirmation, communion, baptism, church membership, church attendance, trying to keep the Ten Commandments, or living out the Sermon on the Mount. It does not come by giving to charity or even by believing that there is a God. It does not come by simply being moral and respectable. Salvation does not even come by claiming to be a Christian. Salvation comes only when we receive by faith the gift of God's grace. Hell will be full of people who tried to reach heaven some other way.

The apostle Paul said, "The law entered that the offense might abound. But where sin abounded, grace abounded much more, so that as sin reigned in death, even so grace might reign through righteousness to eternal life through Jesus Christ our Lord" (Romans 5:20–21). The first provision of the gospel is grace, which is neither earned nor deserved.

Dr. Donald Grey Barnhouse said, "Love that gives upward is worship; love that goes outward is affection; love that stoops is grace." God has stooped to give us grace. Will you receive it?

BY GRACE ALONE

Jesus underscored the truth of salvation only by grace through faith in a provocative interaction with the Pharisees.

John 6 is a record of how all the public goodwill generated by Jesus' miracles gave way to anger and outrage because of the message He proclaimed. The massive crowds dwindled to virtually nothing in the course of a few verses.

Jesus' deity is a major theme in John 6. Jesus' deity became the focus of a previous conflict, too, when He responded to the charge of Sabbath-breaking by claiming the prerogatives of God (John 5:17)—and even claiming that He is worthy of equal honor from all who truly worship God: "so that all will honor the Son even as they honor the Father. He who does not honor the Son does not honor the Father who sent Him" (5:23 NASB). The rest of John 5 is a catalog of witnesses who affirmed Jesus' deity.

John 6 continues with more proofs of Jesus' deity as He feeds the five thousand, walks on water, and declares that He is the bread of life. But the majority of the chapter is devoted to a sermon known as the "Bread of Life discourse."

The setting is important. Jesus had fed the multitudes somewhere on the eastern shore of Galilee, then (walking on water in stormy weather) had gone back to Capernaum (on the northern shore) to get away from the passionate crowd. When word reached Tiberias (on the western shore) about the feeding of the five thousand, many more people came looking for Jesus, hoping for a repeat performance.

The multitudes, now numbering more than five thousand, found Jesus in Capernaum (vv. 24–25, 59).

His message began with a rebuke of their motives: "Most assuredly, I say to you, you seek Me, not because you saw the signs, but because you ate of the loaves and were filled. Do not labor for the food which perishes, but for the food which endures to everlasting life, which the Son of Man will give you, because God the Father has set His seal on Him" (vv. 26–27).

He wanted to talk to them about spiritual things; they were interested mainly in lunch. They began to bargain for a repeat performance of the previous day's miracle. They said they would hear what He had to say *if* He would give them food. As if to put a spiritual spin on the demand, they pointed out that, after all, the manna of Moses' day was literal food that could be eaten: "Our fathers ate the manna in the desert; as it is written, 'He gave them bread from heaven to eat'" (v. 31).

Jesus continued to speak of a different kind of food from heaven—"*true* bread." But, He said, the bread that gives life is a Person, not an edible substance that could be kept in a jar like manna: "For the bread of God is He who comes down from heaven and gives life to the world" (v. 33).

They were still looking for lunch—still seeking a way to feed their physical appetites—when they said, "Lord, give us this bread always" (v. 34).

The back-and-forth dialogue makes a frustrating study in misunderstanding and spiritual blindness.

The voices from the crowd were demanding literal food; Jesus was speaking of something infinitely more important. But they would not see it. There was clearly a tone of testiness and arrogance in their repeated demands (v. 30). It was also obvious that they would not be satisfied with a single encore of the previous day's miracle. "Give us this bread *always*" implies that they wanted Jesus to produce food from heaven every day from then on—like a genie who would magically grant them any wish that struck their fancy. After all, they suggested, that's very much like what Moses did for the Israelites in the wilderness. The manna came every day.

These people were basically offering to make a deal with Jesus: they would believe in Him if He would agree to make food for them from now on, whenever they demanded it.

Jesus certainly *could* have given them food (or anything else they wanted) whenever they wanted. It would have been a very seeker-sensitive way to guarantee that the ranks of His followers would never diminish. Who would not be willing to forsake everything and become His disciple if He could guarantee a life of ease and perpetual food from heaven?

But Jesus was not there to discuss the lunch menu with them, much less barter for their faith by doing miracles on demand. He was going to talk to them about spiritual things. So He said plainly: "I am the bread of life" (v. 35).

That statement instantly brought murmuring protests from the religious leaders in the crowd. They saw clearly that He was claiming to be more than a mere man. They "complained about Him, because He said, 'I am the bread which came down from heaven.' And they said, 'Is not this Jesus, the son of Joseph, whose father and mother we know? How is it then that He says, "I have come down from heaven"'?" (vv. 41–42).

Jesus met their disapproval head-on: "Do not murmur among yourselves. . . . I am the bread of life" (vv. 43, 48). It ought to have been perfectly clear that He was speaking of *spiritual* nourishment and *spiritual* life, because He also said, "He who believes in Me has everlasting life" (v. 47). The doctrine of justification by faith was clearly implied in that statement. He was giving them the very heart of gospel truth, if they had spiritual ears to hear.

He even explained why the true bread of life is superior to Moses' manna: "Your fathers ate the manna in the wilderness, and are dead. This is the bread which comes down from heaven, that one may eat of it and not die" (vv. 49–50). So this bread could give them spiritual life instead of mere physical nourishment, and the bread was Christ Himself. He was clearly explaining a profound spiritual reality, not describing literal food to be ingested by mouth.

John the Baptist had publicly testified that Jesus was the Lamb of God who had come to take away the sin of the world. Jesus' words echoed that prophecy: "The bread that I shall give is My flesh, which I shall give for the life of the world" (v. 51). The words are full of paschal imagery, revealing Christ as the fulfillment of everything the sacrificial system signified. Just as the symbolic Passover lamb was a feast designed to be eaten, Christ (the *true* paschal Lamb) was a spiritual banquet to be received by faith. He was the fulfillment of everything the manna and the Passover feast symbolized, and more.

If the multitudes had shown the least bit of interest in hearing the truth, they would have sought clarification of what they did not understand. Jesus was clearly speaking to them about spiritual realities. From the beginning of this increasingly contentious conversation, they had resisted that and clamored for a free lunch instead. Now they were incapable of thinking in other than literal terms.

"The Jews therefore quarreled among themselves, saying, 'How can this Man give us His flesh to eat?'" (v. 52). Remember that John regularly uses the expression "the Jews" to signify the hostile religious leaders. They were apparently at the head of this crowd.

Notice that Jesus did not stop them at that point and say, "No, you misunderstand. Let me explain what I mean." They had shown no interest in understanding Him, so He persisted with His difficult analogy. In fact, He pressed the metaphor even harder this time: "Most assuredly, I say to you, unless you eat the flesh of the Son of Man and drink His blood, you have no life in you. Whoever eats My flesh and drinks My blood has eternal life, and I will raise him up at the last day. For My flesh is food indeed, and My blood is drink indeed. He who eats My flesh and drinks My blood abides in Me, and I in him" (vv. 53–56). Four times in quick succession He spoke of not only eating His flesh but also drinking His blood.

The symbolic meaning of eating His flesh might have been somewhat transparent to anyone who remembered that the Messiah was the sacrificial lamb who would take away the sin of the world. But when He spoke of drinking His blood, He was using language guaranteed to offend His Jewish audience. The consumption of blood of any kind was deemed grossly unclean under Old Testament law. "You shall not eat the blood of any flesh, for the life of all flesh is its blood. Whoever eats it shall be cut off" (Leviticus 17:14). Kosher food preparation to this day involves carefully removing every trace of blood from meat. In that culture, the idea of consuming blood was considered repulsive in the extreme.

The voices in the crowd had been stubbornly insistent on talking about literal food. The clearer Jesus made it that He was speaking figuratively about spiritual life and spiritual nourishment, the angrier the contrarians became, and the more offensive His words sounded—especially to the Jewish leaders who considered themselves guardians of public piety and ceremonial purity. But finally, even some of Jesus' own disciples began to whisper among themselves, "This is a hard saying; who can understand it?" (v. 60).

Jesus, knowing full well what they were thinking, simply said, "Does this offend you? What then if you should see the Son of Man ascend where He was before? It is the Spirit who gives life; the flesh profits nothing. The words that I speak to you are spirit, and they are life. But there are some of you who do not believe" (vv. 61–64).

Thus He declared plainly that He was using spiritual words to speak of spiritual things. He offered no exegesis of His symbolism and no clarification for the benefit of those who had already become angry with Him. Their failure to grasp His meaning was a fruit of their own disbelief, He said. And John reminds us, "Jesus knew from the beginning who they were who did not believe, and who would betray Him" (v. 64). That, of course, is another echo of John 2:24 ("Jesus did not commit Himself to them, because He knew all men").

It was the end of the discourse. Jesus punctuated it with these words: "Therefore I have said to you that no one can come to Me unless it has been granted to him by My Father" (v. 65). He was referring to an earlier statement, recorded in verse 44: "No one can come to Me unless the Father who sent Me draws him." The implication was that wickedness and rebellion are so deeply ingrained in the character of fallen sinners that apart from divine grace, no one would ever believe.

BY GRACE ARE YOU *SAVED*

The classic text on salvation by grace is Ephesians 2:8–9: "For by grace you have been saved through faith; and that not of yourselves, it is the gift of God; not as a result of works, so that no one should boast" (NASB). Let's look at those verses in their context and try to understand better how Scripture describes the salvation that is by grace through faith in the Lord Jesus Christ.

In Ephesians 1, Paul's central point was God's sovereignty in graciously saving the elect. He wrote that God chose us (v. 4), predestined us (v. 5), guaranteed our adoption (v. 5), bestowed on us His grace (v. 6), redeemed us (v. 7), forgave us (v. 7), lavished riches of grace on us (v. 8), made known to us His will (v. 9), obtained an inheritance for us (v. 11), guaranteed that we would glorify Him (vv. 11–12), saved us (v. 13), and sealed us with the Spirit (vv. 13–14).

In short, He "has blessed us with every spiritual blessing in the heavenly places in Christ" (v. 3). All of this was the work of His sovereign grace, performed not because of any good in us, but simply "according to the kind intention of His will" (vv. 5, 9 NASB) and "according to His purpose who works all things after the counsel of His will" (v. 11 NASB).

Here in the first ten verses of Ephesians 2, Paul chronicled the process of salvation from eternity past:

And you were dead in your trespasses and sins, in which you formerly walked according to the course of this world, according to the prince of the power of the air, of the spirit that is now working in the sons of disobedience. Among them we too all formerly lived in the lusts of our flesh, indulging the desires of the flesh and of the mind, and were by nature children of wrath, even as the rest. But God, being rich in mercy, because of His great love with which He loved us, even when we were dead in our transgressions, made us alive together with Christ (by grace you have been saved), and raised us up with Him, and seated us with Him in the heavenly places, in Christ Jesus, in order that in the ages to come He might show the surpassing riches of His grace in kindness toward us in Christ Jesus. For by grace you have been saved through faith; and that not of yourselves, it is the gift of God; not as a result of works, that no one should boast. For we are His workmanship, created in Christ Jesus for good works, which God prepared beforehand, that we should walk in them. (NASB)

Paul's focus in those verses is solely on *God's* work in saving us, because there is no *human* work to be considered as a part of the saving process (vv. 8–9). These verses describe our past, present, and future as Christians: what we were (vv. 1–3), what we are (vv. 4–6, 8–9), and what we will be (vv. 7, 10). The passage reads like a tract on lordship salvation. The apostle Paul names six features of salvation: it is from sin (vv. 1–3), by love (v. 4), into life (v. 5), for God's glory (vv. 6–7), through faith (vv. 8–9), and unto good works (v. 10).

Salvation for Sinners

Jesus said, "For I did not come to call the righteous, but sinners, to repentance" (Matthew 9:13). Check out Jesus' ancestry in Matthew, and it may surprise you. His genealogy includes some names you might be shocked to find in the royal line of the King of kings. Four women in particular stand out. Not only is it unusual to find women listed in a Hebrew genealogy, but these women are particularly noteworthy because they contrast so dramatically with the absolute purity and righteousness of God's Anointed One. All of them were outcasts, yet they made it into Jesus' family album. They are a strong assurance of God's grace to sinners like us.

You may skip the genealogy when you read the Christmas story aloud. But don't overlook its message of grace, which after all is the heart of the Christmas story: God in His mercy doing for sinners what they cannot do for themselves—mending broken lives and restoring shattered hopes. That's why He came—to save His people from their sins (Matthew 1:21).

Here's the best part: the same grace that was evident in the genealogy is active today, and the same Jesus is saving His people from their sins. No sin, no matter how heinous, puts sinners beyond His reach. "He is able to save them to the uttermost that come unto God by him, seeing he ever liveth to make intercession for them" (Hebrews 7:25 KJV).

Dead in Sin

Paul wrote, "You were dead in your trespasses and sins, in which you formerly walked according to the course of this world, according to the prince of the power of the air, of the spirit that is now working in the sons of disobedience. Among them we too all formerly lived in the lusts of our flesh, indulging the desires of the flesh and of the mind, and were by nature children of wrath, even as the rest" (Ephesians 2:1–3 NASB). There is perhaps no more succinct statement in Scripture on the total depravity and lost condition of sinful mankind.

Because we were born in sin we were born to death, "for the wages of sin is death" (Romans 6:23). People do not become spiritually dead because they sin; they are sinners "by nature" (Ephesians 2:3) and therefore born without spiritual life. Because we were dead to God, we were dead to truth, righteousness, peace, happiness, and every other good thing, no more able to respond to God than a cadaver.

One afternoon early in my ministry at Grace Church I heard a frantic pounding on my office door. I opened the door and there was a little boy, breathless and crying. In a panicked voice he asked, "Are you the reverend?" When I told him I was, he said, "Hurry! Please come with me." It was obvious something was terribly wrong, so I ran with him to his house, about half a block away and across the street from our church. Inside, the boy's mother was weeping uncontrollably. She said, "My baby is dead! My baby is dead!" She quickly took me to a back room. On the bed was the limp body of a tiny infant. He had evidently died in his sleep. The body was blue and already cold to the touch. The mother had been trying desperately to revive him, but nothing could be done. The child was gone. There was absolutely no sign of life. The mother tenderly held the tiny body, kissed him, gently touched his face, spoke to him, and wept over him. But the child made no response. A crew of paramedics arrived and tried to get the child breathing again, but it was too late. Nothing had any effect. There was no response because there was no life. Even the powerful love of a heartbroken mother could not evoke a response.

Spiritual death is exactly like that. Unregenerate sinners have no life by which they can respond to spiritual stimuli. No amount of love, beseeching, or spiritual truth can summon a response. People apart from God are the ungrateful dead, spiritual zombies, death-walkers, unable even to understand the gravity of their situation. They are lifeless. They may go through the motions of life, but they do not possess it. They are dead even while they live (1 Timothy 5:6).

Before salvation every Christian was in precisely the same predicament. None of us responded to God or to His truth. We were "dead in trespasses and sins" (Ephesians 2:1). "We were dead in our transgressions" (v. 5 NASB). "Trespasses and sins" and "transgressions" here do not speak of specific acts. They describe the sphere of existence of the person apart from God, the realm in which sinners live. It is the eternal night of the living dead. All its inhabitants are totally depraved.

Total Depravity

The doctrine of "total depravity" does not mean that every person's lifestyle is equally corrupt and wicked, or that sinners are always as bad as they can be. It means that mankind is corrupt in every regard. The unredeemed are depraved in their minds, their hearts, their wills, their emotions, and their physical beings. They are utterly incapable of anything but sin. Even if they perform humanitarian, philanthropic, or religious deeds, they do them for their own glory, not God's (1 Corinthians 10:31). Sinners may not always sin as grotesquely as possible, but they cannot do anything to please God or earn His favor. Sin has tainted every aspect of their being. That is what it means to be spiritually dead.

A hundred cadavers in the morgue might be in a hundred different phases of decomposition, but they are all equally dead. Depravity, like death, is manifested in many different forms. But just as death itself has no differing degrees of intensity, so depravity is always absolute. Not all people are manifestly as evil as they could be, but all are equally dead in sins.

How do people get around in this state of spiritual death? They walk "according to the course of this world, according to the prince of the power of the air, the spirit who now works in the sons of disobedience" (Ephesians 2:2). Satan is "the prince of the power of the air." He governs the realm of sin and death ("this world") in which the unredeemed function. It is a realm that features many different and apparently competing religions, moral systems, and standards of behavior, but ultimately they are all under the control and in the grip of the devil. "The whole world lies in the power of the evil one" (1 John 5:19 NASB).

Thus the unredeemed—whether they realize it or not—have a common lord, "the prince of the power of the air." Satan is the *archoμn*, the prince. He is "the ruler of this world" and will reign until the Lord casts him out (John 12:31). All those in this realm of sin and death live under his dominion, share his nature, are conspirators in his rebellion against God, and so respond naturally to his authority. They are on the same spiritual wavelength. Jesus even calls the devil the father of those under his lordship (John 8:44).

Note that the unsaved are "by nature children of wrath" (Ephesians 2:3). People are not "all God's children," as some are fond of saying. Those who have not received salvation through Jesus Christ are God's enemies (Romans 5:10; 8:7; James 4:4), not only "sons of disobedience," but consequently "children of wrath"—objects of God's eternal condemnation.

Paul's purpose in Ephesians 2:1–3 is not to show how unsaved people live—though the teaching is valuable for that purpose—but to remind believers how they *previously* lived. All of us "*formerly* lived in the lusts of our flesh, indulging the desires of the flesh and of the mind, and were by nature children of wrath, even as the rest" (v. 3 NASB, emphasis added). The realm of sin and death is a past-tense experience for the believer.

We *were* hopelessly subject to the world, the flesh, and the devil (vv. 2–3). We *formerly* walked as sons of disobedience (v. 2). We *were* dead in sins and trespasses (v. 1). Now all that is in the past. Although we were once like the rest of mankind, by God's grace we are no longer like that. Because of His saving work in us, we are presently and eternally redeemed. We have been delivered from spiritual death, sin, alienation from God, disobedience, demon control, lust, and divine judgment (vv. 1–3). That is what saving grace accomplishes.

SIN AND SINNERS

As much as God hates sin, He loves sinners. Set against the dark background of our sin, the grace of God becomes all the more wondrous. The most familiar passage in all Scripture is John 3:16. Without an understanding of the wickedness of sin, however, we cannot grasp the tremendous significance of this verse: "For God so loved the world that He gave His only begotten Son, that whoever believes in Him should not perish but have eternal life."

- *"God so loved . . ."* Why would God love me despite my sin?
- *"God so loved the world . . ."* Why would God love a whole world of sinners?

- *"God so loved the world that He gave His only begotten Son . . ."* Why would God's love for sinners be so compelling as to make Him sacrifice His beloved Son in such agony and humiliation?

- *"God so loved the world that He gave His only begotten Son, that whoever believes in Him . . ."* Why would God make salvation so simple for sinners, requiring only faith of us, and having done all the necessary expiatory work Himself?

- *"God so loved the world that He gave His only begotten Son, that whoever believes in Him should not perish . . ."* Why would God want to exempt sinners from the judgment they themselves deserve, even to the point of allowing His only begotten Son to accept that judgment on behalf of those who do not deserve His mercy?

- *"God so loved the world that He gave His only begotten Son, that whoever believes in Him should not perish but have eternal life."* Why would God want to give everlasting life in His presence to sinners who have done nothing but oppose Him and hate Him?

The answer is found in *God's grace.* "God, being rich in mercy, because of His great love with which He loved us, even when we were dead in our transgressions, made us alive together with Christ (by grace you have been saved)" (Ephesians 2:4–5 NASB). "The wages of sin is death, but the gift of God is eternal life in Christ Jesus our Lord" (Romans 6:23). "Blessed are those whose lawless deeds have been forgiven, and whose sins have been covered. Blessed is the man whose sin the Lord will not take into account" (Romans 4:7–8 NASB).

A BRILLIANT CONCESSION

In Luke 4:24, in His interaction with the Jewish leaders in the local synagogue, Jesus said, "Assuredly, I say to you, no prophet is accepted in his own country." Instead of "Assuredly," some translations retain "Amen" from the Greek, meaning "I solemnly assure you." It's an idiom for "I'm telling you the truth. No prophet is welcome in his hometown; no prophet is *dektos*, accepted, in his hometown." Experts are always from out of town, aren't they? It's yet more proof that familiarity breeds contempt.

Jesus was making a bit of a concession. He was saying to them in so many words, "I can see it's hard for you to get past the fact that I'm a local guy, that I grew up here, that I am Joseph's son and Mary's boy, and that this is the synagogue you have seen Me in all the years of My life. I understand that." I think there's a bit of mercy in Jesus' words of understanding that no prophet is welcome in his hometown. He repeated that phrase a year and a half later, when He came back again to that synagogue, as recorded in Matthew 13:57 and Mark 6:4. It also appears in John 4:44.

Jesus made this concession in the light of human behavior being what it is. But then He made a brilliant and profound transition. He brought up two prophets, Elijah in Luke 4:25 and Elisha in verse 27, whom the people of Israel had hated, rejected, and refused. Jesus' hearers all knew of Elijah, the great prophet of Israel. During his ministry around 850 BC, there were many widows. Moreover, Baal worship was going on everywhere because the king, Ahab, had married a pagan Baal worshipper named Jezebel. Ahab began worshipping Baal under the influence of his wife, and soon the whole of Israel followed his example. Ahab was so bad, 1 Kings 16:33 says, that he "did more to provoke the LORD God of Israel to anger than all the kings of Israel who were before him."

Chapter 17 of 1 Kings begins with the prophet Elijah calling down the judgment of God upon Ahab and his subjects. Elijah prayed to the true God for a drought to prove that Baal, Ahab's god of rain and fertility, was a powerless god, false and impotent. God answered Elijah with a drought that lasted three and a half years. In Luke 4:25–26, Jesus reminded His listeners of the fact that God sent Elijah to a destitute widow in the town of Zarephath at the height of the drought, and he told her in the name of the Lord that if she shared the last of her food with him, the Lord would supply all her needs until the rains returned. She was obedient to the true God, despite having only enough flour and oil for one meager, final meal for herself and her son. She gave Elijah the food he requested.

This was a life-and-death decision for her. With no other support, she expected to starve after they had eaten the last morsels in the house. Sharing what little they had with this stranger would bring them to their desperate end even sooner. Yet, because she was obedient, God showed her His mercy, and from then until the drought was over, He miraculously replenished her flour bin and oil jar every day.

This story infuriated the Jews, because the widow of Zarephath was a Gentile in a culture that worshipped Baal, yet God bypassed many needy widows in Israel and sent Elijah only to this woman, who had made no effort at all to observe the religious laws with which the Israelites were so obsessed. It was her individual faith in the true God that mattered, not her tribal or religious pedigree. How was that possible? How could God bless a despicable Gentile in a pagan land, while seeming to ignore the law-abiding Jews? Outrageous!

Though the people in the synagogue were getting angrier by the moment, Jesus kept the truth coming. He went on in verse 27 to a story about Elisha, who succeeded Elijah, during a time from 850 to 790 BC, when many lepers were in Israel. Leprosy was a sort of categorical word that covered a variety of ancient diseases that affected the skin described in Leviticus 13, everything from superficial problems to serious ones. It may also have included what we today call leprosy, that frightening malady also known as Hansen's disease.

These tended to be disfiguring diseases, and some could spread frighteningly fast. They made the victims unclean; they were cut off from all fellowship, social activity, and family contact, and they were isolated because others feared being stricken (though today with modern treatment, the risk of spreading Hansen's disease is considered negligible). Israel had many, many such rank outcasts, physically quarantined for their horrible maladies. It was in the time of Elisha, and they didn't like Elisha. He had no more honor in his own country than Elijah did. The people were still worshipping Baal, they were still turning their backs on the true and living God, and then along came leprosies everywhere. And Luke 4:27 says that God cleansed none of the lepers except Naaman the Syrian.

Oh man, did the Jews hate this story! Naaman was a military commander in chief of a land known as

Aram. He commanded terrorists who were always pillaging Israel. They crossed the border, carried out their raid, killed Jews, and took men and women prisoners back to Syria to use as slaves. Naaman was a violent enemy leader, like the modern Palestinian militants who attack the Jews. What's more, he was a Gentile, and he was a leper! He was about as despicable as people get.

On one of his raids, described in 2 Kings 5, he captured a girl and brought her back to be a slave to his wife. Amazingly, the girl had a compassionate attitude: she knew about his leprosy, and she told him he needed to go to Israel to find the man of God named Elisha, because God could heal through him. Naaman began to believe in the power of the God of Israel, and eventually, through a series of events, he wound up meeting Elisha.

Elisha said the God of Israel would heal Naaman if he immersed himself in the river seven times. The suggestion made Naaman furious. Here was a prideful figure who saw himself as a VIP, a man of great honor, a military leader of stature, dignity, and nobility. No way was he going to be demeaned by dunking himself seven times. He even complained at the thought of going in Elisha's dirty river, when he had a nice clean river back home.

But Naaman left Elisha's house and his servant said, "Well, better a dirty river and a clean Naaman, huh?" He started to have second thoughts. And he realized his desperation, realized that there was no relief and no cure, no healing except by the God of Israel. *Is this man of God really the man of God? Is God truly God? Is Elisha really His prophet?* Naaman was thinking, *How will I ever know unless I submit to what He asks? In my desperation, my destitution, and my disease, I have to do what the man tells me to do. Then I'll know whether he's the man of God and Israel's God is the True Deliverer.*

So he went and did his seven dunks in Elisha's dirty river. Guess what? He was washed clean from every element of his leprosy!

If you were sitting in the synagogue at that moment, you were saying, "This is not going well. So we are worse than a Gentile widow from Jezebel's hometown! We are worse than a Syrian Gentile terrorist leper! This is intolerable! God overlooks our widows and lepers and shows His grace to pagans. And He's going to pass us by now, if we don't embrace Jesus as Lord and Messiah."

SALVATION IS BY LOVE

God's grace extends to outcasts and lepers, to us. So great is His love.

"But God, who is rich in mercy, because of His great love with which He loved us . . . made us alive together with Christ" (Ephesians 2:4–5). God's mercy is "rich," measureless, overflowing, abundant, unlimited. Some who struggle with the concept of sovereign grace believe God is unfair to elect some and not save everyone. That is exactly opposite from right thinking. The truth is, *everyone* deserves hell. God in His grace elects to save some. *No one* would be saved apart from God's sovereign grace. The thing that keeps sinners from being reconciled to God is not a deficiency of mercy or grace on God's side of the equation. It is *sin*, and sin is a problem. Rebellion and rejection are in the nature of every sinner.

The two words "but God" affirm that the initiative to save is all God's. Because He is rich in mercy toward us, and because of His great love for us, He intervened and provided a way by grace for us to return to Him.

God is intrinsically kind, merciful, and loving. Love is so integral to who He is that the apostle John wrote, "God is love" (1 John 4:8, 16). In His love He reaches out to sinful, corrupt, impoverished, condemned, spiritually dead human beings and blesses them with every spiritual blessing in the heavenly places in Christ (Ephesians 1:3).

Not only does God love enough to forgive but also enough to give His Son to die for the very ones who had offended Him: "God so loved the world that He gave His only begotten Son, that whoever believes in

Him should not perish but have eternal life" (John 3:16). "Greater love has no one than this, that one lay down his life for his friends" (John 15:13 NASB). God's love for those who do not deserve it makes salvation possible and fills salvation with every mercy. It is the epitome of sovereign grace.

THE THRILL OF GRACE

Is the experience of God's grace in your life a thrilling thing? It is for me! Just thinking about the fact that God, by His own sovereign plan, decided to be gracious to me is overwhelming.

He poured out His grace on me. He forgave all my sins. He granted me the indwelling of the Holy Spirit. He gave me an understanding of His Word. He called me to spiritual ministry. Every day He gives me a rich communion with the saints, and I relish being a part of His redeemed people. He enables me to see the world as His handiwork. I am His child, and He loves me in a personal way.

There is nothing greater than receiving grace upon grace. I pray that is your experience.

CHAPTER 3

Grace Misunderstood and Twisted

Through the years, Arminian and Calvinistic theologies have been at opposite poles. Traditional Reformed theology, which we call Calvinism, emphasizes God's sovereignty, but Arminian theology in effect emphasizes man's sovereignty. It teaches that God is helpful in providing spiritual assistance, but that one must find it in himself to come to Christ, persevere in the faith, accomplish spiritual goals, and win spiritual victories.

What results from that kind of theology? A person can profess to trust in Christ, but in reality trusts in himself. This reflects the belief that the power to choose salvation—or lose it through spiritual failure—belongs to the individual. Suppose you believed you had that kind of power. Can you imagine what it would be like to face death and wonder if you would be disqualified from heaven because you had committed too many sins? That kind of uncertainty will bring anxiety, not security.

Fully trusting God requires an understanding of His sovereign grace: that an individual is chosen, redeemed, kept, and glorified by God, who is the initiator.

TWO RELIGIONS

Humanity has always had two systems of religion available. One is from God and is based on His gracious accomplishment. The other is from mankind and is based on the achievements of men and women. One is all sovereign grace and is embraced by faith. The other is all human works and is performed in the flesh. One flows out of a sincere heart, the other from outward hypocrisy.

Even Moses' law, though from God, was not a means of salvation. It was a means of showing people their need for salvation. "Therefore by the deeds of the law no flesh will be justified in His sight, for by the law is the knowledge of sin" (Romans 3:20). When Jesus came, He taught us that we are incapable in ourselves of keeping that perfect law. He made it clear that we must choose the religion of grace and faith rather than the religion of law and works.

SALVATION BY FAITH ALONE

Let's return to this key passage: "For by grace you have been saved through faith, and that not of yourselves; it is the gift of God, not of works, lest anyone should boast" (Ephesians 2:8–9). Here we see that faith is our *response*, not the *cause* of salvation. Even faith is "not of ourselves"; it is included in "the gift of God."

Some object to this interpretation. They point out that *faith* (*pistis*) is feminine, while *that* (*touto*) is neuter. Grammatically, the pronoun *that* has no clear antecedent. It refers not to the noun, *faith*, but more likely to the (understood) act of believing. It could possibly refer to the whole of salvation.

Either way, the meaning is inescapable: faith is God's gracious gift. Jesus explicitly affirmed this truth: "No one can come to Me, unless it has been granted him from the Father" (John 6:65 NASB). Faith is also spoken of as a divine gift in Acts 3:16: "The faith which comes through Him has given him this perfect health in the presence of you all" (NASB); Philippians 1:29: "To you it has been granted for Christ's sake, not only to believe in Him, but also to suffer for His sake" (NASB); and 2 Peter 1:1: "Simon Peter, a bond-servant and apostle of Jesus Christ, to those who have received a faith of the same kind as ours" (NASB).

"Not by works" is not contrasting faith versus repentance, faith versus commitment, or faith versus surrender. In fact, the issue here is not as simple as faith versus circumcision or faith versus baptism. The contrast is between *divine grace* and *human merit*.

Human effort cannot bring salvation. We are saved by grace alone through faith alone in Christ alone. When we relinquish all hope except faith in Christ and

His finished work on our behalf, we are acting by the faith that God in His grace supplies. Believing is therefore the first act of an awakened spiritual corpse; it is the new man drawing his first breath. Because faith is unfailing, the spiritual man keeps on breathing.

Obviously, if salvation is entirely by God's grace, it cannot be as a result of works. Human effort has nothing to do with gaining or sustaining it (Romans 3:20; Galatians 2:16). No one should boast, as if we had any part in bringing it about (Romans 3:27; 4:5; 1 Corinthians 1:31).

FAITH WITHOUT WORKS

Although salvation is by grace alone through faith alone, our faith does not stand alone. Yet that's what some seem to teach, the idea that people simply need to raise a hand, walk an aisle, say a prayer, and that's it—they're in. This is "cheap grace," and it flies in the face of James 2:26: "For as the body without the spirit is dead, so faith without works is dead also." True faith, genuine commitment to Christ, results in "works." A changed heart results in a changed life.

Fuzzy Faith

It should come as no surprise that, at this point in time, the enemy of men's souls—God's archenemy,

Satan himself—has cranked up his efforts to prevent the spread of the gospel. One of his prime tactics is to make the church confused about what the gospel is. It docsn't do any good to have this fantastic contemporary communication technology, or wealth, manpower, and passion to take the gospel message to the ends of the earth, if you don't know what the gospel message is. So it's certainly a wise strategy on the part of the enemy of men's souls to confuse the church about the message.

Along with many others, I have been preaching, teaching, and writing to try and clarify for Christians what the gospel is. They're not really sure whether Jesus is Lord or not, or whether He *needs* to be Lord or not. It doesn't seem to be important these days that people understand the true biblical doctrine of justification by faith alone, through grace alone, in Christ alone. It doesn't seem to matter to some people that there be repentance of sin, and that we preach repentance. In fact, some people think the idea of repentance is an intrusion into grace. They fail to comprehend the doctrine of substitution and imputation, which is the true understanding that God imputed (meaning ascribed or assigned) our sins fully to a substitute who died in our place, and that we contribute nothing to our salvation but lay hold of eternal life by faith in that substitute.

Seeker-Sensitive

"Seeker-sensitive" churches have sprouted up across our land, and many have become mega-churches. Often a part of what makes them attractive to outsiders is the message that following Christ is easy—easy to get in (no repentance needed) and easy to live out.

What happens at a seeker-sensitive church when somebody takes the bait? He thinks, *Hey, this Christianity thing is not hard at all. Meet nice people, hear an inspiring message and some cool music, get to heaven.* But at some point the truth comes out. The hard words of Jesus come out: "It's not about you; it's about Me and sacrificing yourself to follow Me."

It's absolutely true that nobody's going to want to be a Christian under those circumstances, *unless the Spirit of God is working in his heart.* Unless the Spirit of God is doing the work of conviction, is awakening the dead heart, and generating faith, nothing's going to happen, *no matter what you do.* And then *only the true message of Jesus, connected with the work of the Spirit, will produce true salvation.* The fountain of grace will open and flow to the self-denying sinner. This is the very essence of grace. It is when we offer nothing in ourselves as worthy of salvation, but affirm our hatred of our worthless self, that God grants us grace to rescue us from sin and hell.

We can't reinvent the gospel to suit ourselves,

our own comfort and convenience. But that's what people are doing today. If you modify the message to make Christianity more attractive, then what you have is not Christianity.

I'm not promoting legalism in any form, only fidelity to Scripture, though some people have decided I'm sort of harsh and hard-nosed. One well-known evangelical friend thought he was complimenting me when he introduced me by saying, "This is John MacArthur, who is much nicer in person than he is in his books."

I smiled and said, "In person it's much easier to demonstrate the love of Christ."

A COMMON MISCONCEPTION

A common misconception has the choice between Christ and false gods as the choice between desiring to go to hell and desiring to go to heaven. I've heard preachers say the narrow way is the way of Christianity that people choose when they want to go to heaven, and the broad way is the way people choose who are content to go to hell. But they are misinformed or confused. It is not a contrast between godliness and Christianity on one hand and irreligious, lewd, lascivious pagan masses headed merrily for hell on the other. It is a contrast between two kinds of religions, both roads marked "This Way to Heaven." Satan doesn't put up a sign that says, "Hell—Exit Here." That's not his style. People on the broad road think that road goes to heaven.

It's also a contrast between divine righteousness and human righteousness, between divine religion and human religion, thus between true religion and false religion. God's Word described the Pharisees' problem in Luke 18:9, which says that they "trusted in themselves that they were righteous." It was a religion of human righteousness. They worshipped themselves. And that was inadequate, because they weren't righteous enough to meet the high standard of God's kingdom. Only Jesus can do that.

The choice we all make is this: either we're good enough on our own, through our belief system and morality, to make it to heaven; or we're not, and we have to cast ourselves on the mercy of God through Christ to get there. Those are the only two systems of religion in the world. One is a religion of human merit; the other recognizes that we find true merit in Christ alone, and it comes to the sinner only by grace. There may be a thousand different religious names and terms, but only two religions really exist. There is the truth of divine accomplishment, which says God has done it all in Christ, and there is the lie of human achievement, which says we have some sort of hand in saving ourselves. One is the religion of grace, the other the religion of works. One offers salvation by faith alone; the other offers salvation by the flesh.

THE BROAD WAY TO DESTRUCTION

Jesus spoke clearly about this false idea of how one can be saved. The final plea of His Sermon on the Mount is a general invitation to "enter by the narrow gate; for wide is the gate and broad is the way that leads to destruction, and there are many who go in by it. Because narrow is the gate and difficult is the way which leads to life, and there are few who find it" (Matthew 7:13–14). The narrow gate and difficult road are references to the gospel's demand for total self-denial and humility—and all the other qualities highlighted in the beatitudes.

Proud and unbroken sinners always choose the wrong road. That's why it is full of travelers. It's broad enough for everyone, from out-and-out libertines to the strictest Pharisees. All of them like it, because no one has to bow low or leave any baggage behind in order get on this highway. Furthermore, all the road signs promise heaven. There's just one problem, and it's a significant one: the road does not actually go to heaven. It leads instead to utter destruction.

Furthermore, Jesus says, the world is full of false prophets who steer people onto the broad road. Beware of them. They "come to you in sheep's clothing, but inwardly they are ravenous wolves" (Matthew 7:15). He might well be painting a verbal portrait of the Pharisees. This is, in fact, a generic description of *all* false prophets in all ages, but the religious elite of Israel epitomized everything He was talking about. That fact was surely not lost on them, or on the general audience.

"You will know them by their fruits," Jesus said (Matthew 7:16). The imagery of bad trees with bad fruit had special significance for the Pharisees. Some Pharisees and Sadducees had come to John the Baptist not many months before this. Apparently they saw how popular John was, and they wanted the admiration of his followers. John called them the offspring of vipers and told them to "bear fruits worthy of repentance" (Matthew 3:7–8). Then he added, "Even now the ax is laid to the root of the trees. Therefore every tree which does not bear good fruit is cut down and thrown into the fire" (v. 10)—and began to prophesy about Jesus.

Now, in wrapping up His Sermon on the Mount, Jesus employed the very same imagery, and even quoted John the Baptist's exact words: "Every good tree bears good fruit, but a bad tree bears bad fruit. A good tree cannot bear bad fruit, nor can a bad tree bear good fruit. *Every tree that does not bear good fruit is cut down and thrown into the fire.* Therefore by their fruits you will know them" (Matthew 7:17–20, emphasis added). Those were strong words of condemnation, and though Jesus' admonition was not limited to religious leaders, no one could possibly miss the fact that Jesus was treading directly on the toes of the Pharisees and Sadducees.

A MESSAGE FOR THE MASSES

Nevertheless, it would be wrong to conclude that the Sermon on the Mount was only—or even *mainly*—preached for the benefit of Israel's hypocritical religious leaders. While the Pharisees and Sadducees epitomized the hypocrisy and self-righteousness Jesus targeted, they were by no means the only ones with whom He was pleading. He was speaking to everyone on the broad road. His description of the judgment that awaits at the end of that road is chilling:

> Not everyone who says to Me, "Lord, Lord," shall enter the kingdom of heaven, but he who does the will of My Father in heaven. Many will say to Me in that day, "Lord, Lord, have we not prophesied in Your name, cast out demons in Your name, and done many wonders in Your name?"

And then I will declare to them, "I never knew you; depart from Me, you who practice lawlessness!" Therefore whoever hears these sayings of Mine, and does them, I will liken him to a wise man who built his house on the rock: and the rain descended, the floods came, and the winds blew and beat on that house; and it did not fall, for it was founded on the rock. But everyone who hears these sayings of Mine, and does not do them, will be like a foolish man who built his house on the sand: and the rain descended, the floods came, and the winds blew and beat on that house; and it fell. And great was its fall. (Matthew 7:21–27)

The word *many* echoes through the passage. *Many* go in by the wide gate onto the broad road (Matthew 7:13). *Many* will say "Have we not . . . done *many* wonders?" (v. 22). But notice: It's not merely Pharisees and Sadducees who will try to argue at the judgment seat that their works ought to be sufficient to get them into heaven. Jesus was describing people who profess to be Christians. They call Jesus "Lord, Lord." They claim to have done mighty works *in His name*.

But He sends them away with these soul-shattering words: "I never knew you; depart from Me." So it turns out the Sermon on the Mount is not a message just for the Pharisees, even though Jesus attacked their beliefs from the start of the sermon through its conclusion. The underlying message is chiefly for disciples, and it is a warning to them, lest they fall into the very same errors that turned the Pharisees' religion into a monstrosity that was odious to God and made them hostile to the truth.

MORE HARD WORDS
FOR DISCIPLES

Those final words from the Sermon on the Mount left people breathless. They "were astonished at His teaching, for He taught them as one having authority, and not as the scribes" (Matthew 7:28–29). The Pharisees could not teach without citing this or that rabbi and resting on the pedigree of centuries-long traditions. Their religion was academic in practically every sense of that word. And to many of them, teaching was just another opportunity to seek praise from men—by showing off their erudition. They took great pride in citing as many sources as possible, carefully footnoting their sermons. They were more concerned with what others said about the law than they were with what the law itself actually taught. They had thus learned the law without ever really listening to it (Galatians 4:21).

Jesus, by contrast, quoted no authority other than the Word of God itself. He gave its interpretation without buttressing His point of view with endless quotations from earlier writers. If He cited religious scholars at all, it was to refute them. He spoke as one who *has* authority, because He does. He is God, and His style of delivery reflected that. His words were full of love and tenderness toward repentant sinners—but equally full of hard sayings and harsh-sounding words for the self-righteous and self-satisfied. As we have seen from the start, He wasn't inviting an exchange of opinions, giving an academic lecture, or looking for common cause with the religious leaders of the land; He was declaring the Word of God *against* them.

HOLINESS: NOT AN OPTION

God's grace does not mean holiness is optional. There have always been people who abuse God's grace by assuming it grants leeway for sin. Paraphrasing that philosophy, Paul wrote, "What shall we say then? Are we to continue in sin so that grace might increase?" (Romans 6:1 NASB). If grace abounds most where sin is worst (Romans 5:20–21), then doesn't our sin only magnify the grace of God? Should we continue in sin so that God's grace can be magnified?

"May it never be!" Paul answered in a phrase so emphatic that the King James Version renders it "God forbid!" The notion that anyone would use such an argument to condone sin was clearly offensive to Paul. "How shall we who died to sin still live in it?" (Romans 6:2 NASB).

DEALING WITH FALSE TEACHERS

Some lay people and pastors may simply misunderstand God's message of salvation by grace alone, through faith alone, and those certainly can pose a danger. But others, what the Bible calls "false teachers," lie, deliberately twisting the truth.

In the small epistle of Jude, we find Jesus' brother urging believers to "contend earnestly for the faith" as he warns them about "ungodly men, who turn the grace of our God into lewdness and deny the only Lord God and our Lord Jesus Christ" (vv. 3–4).

Remember, Jude is writing about apostates and gospel corrupters. He is not suggesting that every trivial flaw in someone's thinking about nonessential or difficult doctrines is an occasion to bring out the heavy weapons. He is certainly not exhorting us to get militant every time there is a disagreement in the church. Sometimes, even close friends and true brothers in Christ disagree sharply. In such cases, if reconciliation proves impossible, parting company amicably is preferable to a fight (Acts 15:37–41). As the Old Testament sage reminds us, there is "a time to keep silence, and a time to speak; a time to love, and a time to hate; a time of war, and a time of peace" (Ecclesiastes 3:7–8).

Honest disagreements between true brethren should never escalate into mortal combat (Psalm 133:1; John 13:35; 1 Corinthians 1:10; Ephesians 4:3–6). Jude's call to battle applies when there is a serious threat to "the faith which was once for all delivered to the saints" (v. 3)—the kind of false teaching that undermines the foundations of the gospel. The error Jude had in mind did not stem from some slight misunderstanding about a difficult text. He was talking about heresy that is ultimately rooted in willful unbelief—a denial of "the only Lord God and our Lord Jesus Christ" (Jude v. 4).

He had in mind an error that corrupts the essential character of the gospel. He was talking about *damnable* error. He stressed that fact when he said the purveyors of such heresies are destined for condemnation. Now, bear in mind that such errors are often subtle and hard to spot. The only way to develop the discernment necessary for detecting such subtle error and correctly assessing its danger is by applying oneself conscientiously to the task of rightly dividing the Word of God (2 Timothy 2:15). That skill must be perfected over time through faithful diligence.

Furthermore, as I have stressed from the start, apostates are usually clandestine about their unbelief.

The mere fact that someone professes to be a brother in Christ and insists that he is only making negligible and perfectly benign doctrinal distinctions does not make It so. In fact, that is exactly what Jude is describing: false teachers who deliberately try to remain unnoticed—who *pretend* loyalty to Christ, but whose doctrine contradicts that profession. It can be quite difficult to see past someone's phony profession of faith and assess the true gravity of his error. That is one of the main reasons harsh judgments are not to be made lightly. "Do not judge according to appearance, but *judge with righteous judgment*" (John 7:24, emphasis added).

But that verse (often erroneously cited as an argument for withholding all judgments completely) is actually the opposite: a *command* to judge righteously. We can't set aside all judgment just because discernment is difficult. Willful gullibility is disobedience to God's Word. "Do not believe every spirit, but test the spirits, whether they are of God; because many false prophets have gone out into the world" (1 John 4:1).

Still, overzealousness is clearly a danger we need to guard against carefully. There are indeed some full-time critics operating today, always looking for a fight, taking fleshly delight in controversy merely for controversy's sake, and making judgments that may be too harsh or too hasty. Don't fall into the trap of assuming that the most censorious and nitpicking opinions are automatically the most "discerning" ones. Watch out for the person who shows no caution or restraint about making severe judgments and yet claims to be a discernment expert. True discernment is gained by applying our hearts and minds to biblical wisdom, not by fostering a critical spirit.

As a matter of fact, Scripture says that those who are merely pugnacious or quarrelsome are unfit for spiritual leadership (1 Timothy 3:3). When Paul laid out the qualifications for church leaders, he was emphatic about this. "A servant of the Lord must not quarrel but be gentle to all, able to teach, patient, in humility correcting those who are in opposition, if God perhaps will grant them repentance, so that they may know the truth" (2 Timothy 2:24–25). That is the spirit we must cultivate. Contending earnestly for the faith does not require us to become brawlers. Let's acknowledge that as plainly as possible and never lose sight of it.

But by far the greater danger facing the church today is utter apathy toward the truth and indifference about false teaching. Frankly, we are not very good these days at guarding the truth. We tend not to see truth the way Scripture presents it—as a sacred treasure committed to our trust (1 Timothy 6:20–21). I think that is why evangelicals on the whole don't take seriously the duty to expose and refute false teachers. Too many have decided it is easier and seems so much "nicer" to pretend that every doctrinal deviation is ultimately insignificant. That kind of thinking has given Christians a dangerous sense of false comfort and security.

HOW TO SPOT AN APOSTATE

Jude seems to suggest that the church in his day had been lulled into a similar state of deadly apathy, and the false teachers were having a heyday because of it. Perhaps that is why his warning sounds so shrill.

In fact, the sharpness of the warning is suited to the danger posed by the purveyors of heresy. As we shall shortly observe, their ungodliness had multiple dimensions.

Ungodly is one of the key words in Jude's epistle. In verse 15 alone, he used the word four times. The Lord is coming, he said, "to execute judgment on all, to convict all who are *ungodly* among them of all their *ungodly* deeds which they have committed in an *ungodly* way, and of all the harsh things which *ungodly* sinners have spoken against Him" (emphasis added). In verse 4 he used the word as a general description of the apostates themselves.

This is their chief characteristic: they were un-godly. They were without God. They were godless in their thoughts, their affections, and their doctrine.

They claimed to belong to God, to represent God, and to speak for God. But of all the lies they told, that was probably the most glaringly untrue. They were actually ungodly—without any real love or obedience in their hearts toward the true God.

Jude then pointed out two major ways the ungodliness of the false teachers was manifest:

Their Character

First, Jude candidly referred to the false teachers as "ungodly men" (v. 4). That was his assessment of their character. They had no integrity, were not men of principle, and were utterly lacking in all the fruits of true godliness. They were without any actual reverence for God and evidenced no true love for Him. They were barren of any authentic holiness. Aside from their phony profession of faith in Christ, they had no vital connection to Him whatsoever. They certainly did not reflect any degree of Christlikeness in their character. They simply played at religion.

Their Conduct

Second, these "ungodly men . . . turn[ed] the grace of our God into lewdness" (v. 4). That means they presumptuously regarded God's kindness to sinners as a license for immoral conduct. They talked a lot about "grace" and promised "liberty," but they themselves were slaves of corruption (2 Peter 2:19).

All their stress on freedom in Christ was actually a backhanded assault on God's grace. Grace to them was nothing more than a phony justification for lust-driven behavior.

Jude v. 18 echoes the same charge, again using the key word *ungodly* as a description of the false teachers' character: they "walk according to their own ungodly lusts."

Get the picture here: these were seriously ungodly men, and they were in the church. They were teaching and influencing people with nice-sounding words about grace and freedom in Christ, while in reality they were driven by their own unbridled lust and evil desires. Nevertheless, they gained a following in the church.

We must not be naive. Evil apostates like that are still in the church today. Their ungodliness is not always instantly evident. Some try to hide it under religious robes, divert attention from it by affecting kindliness or congeniality, or mask it with some other superficial kind of piety. They work hard to keep up the spiritual facade, but their true character is ungodly, and they cannot ultimately suppress the inevitable fruit of that. "The works of the flesh are *evident*, which are: adultery, fornication, uncleanness, lewdness, idolatry, sorcery, hatred, contentions, jealousies, outbursts of wrath, selfish ambitions, dissensions, heresies, envy, murders, drunkenness, revelries, and the like" (Galatians 5:19–21, emphasis added).

The ungodliness of an apostate system will occasionally become gross, widespread, and scandalous. A network of pedophile priests, for example—carefully camouflaged under a methodical cover-up that has been orchestrated by the church hierarchy—is a pretty clear sign of a system shot through with apostasy. No amount of clerical garb can mask the evil in that.

But the fruits of apostasy and ungodliness are not necessarily that obvious. Apostates are not unique to any single denomination or theological system. They are by no means limited to cults and fringe groups. On the contrary, they often deliberately conceal themselves within the heart of the evangelical mainstream. Some teach in evangelical seminaries and Bible colleges. Some pastor churches.

How is their ungodly character manifest? In worldly lifestyles and unwholesome preoccupations. In private behavior that contradicts the carefully crafted public image. In sensual talk and carnal conduct. In the kind of hypocrisy that practices religion merely for the praise of men but cares not about pleasing God (Matthew 6:1–8).

CHAPTER 4

GRACE REALIZED

Because justification is by faith alone, through grace alone, in Christ alone, here are the personal realities.

SALVATION IS LIFE

Paul asserted, "Even when we were dead in our transgressions, [God] made us alive together with Christ" (Ephesians 2:5 NASB). The saving transaction begins the moment God gives spiritual life to a dead person. It is God who makes the first move. Jesus said, "No one can come to Me unless the Father who sent Me draws him" (John 6:44). Of course! The unsaved are *dead*, incapable of any spiritual activity. Until God quickens us, we have no capacity to respond to Him in faith.

When sinners are saved, they are no longer alienated from the life of God. They become spiritually alive through a miraculous, God-wrought union with Christ. They become sensitive to God for the first time. Paul calls it "newness of life" (Romans 6:4). Now they understand spiritual truth and desire spiritual things (1 Corinthians 2:10–16). Now they become partakers of the divine nature (2 Peter 1:4).

They can pursue godliness—"the things above"— rather than "the things that are on earth" (Colossians 3:2 NASB).

This new life is "in Christ Jesus" (Ephesians 2:6). He *is* our life (Colossians 3:4). "We . . . live with Him" (Romans 6:8), in the likeness of His resurrection (Romans 6:5). Our new life is actually His life lived in us (Galatians 2:20). It is utterly different from our former life and the supreme manifestation of God's sovereign grace.

FOR GOD'S GLORY

"[God] raised us up with Him, and seated us with Him in the heavenly places, in Christ Jesus, in order that in the ages to come He might show the surpassing riches of His grace in kindness toward us in Christ Jesus" (Ephesians 2:6–7 NASB). Salvation has a particular purpose: that we might enjoy and display His glory, showing forth the riches of His grace (Romans 9:23).

Our new citizenship is in heaven (Philippians 3:20). God raises us up with Christ and seats us with Him in the heavenly places. We no longer belong to this present world or its sphere of sinfulness and rebellion. We are rescued from spiritual death and the consequences of our sin. That is pure grace.

Note that the apostle describes this heavenly life

as if it were already fully accomplished. Even though we are not yet in full possession of all that God has for us in Christ, we live in His domain, just as we formerly lived in the realm of sin and death. "Heavenly places" clearly implies the full sense of God's dominion. This expression cannot be read in a way that makes His lordship optional.

To dwell in the heavenly domain is to enjoy full fellowship with the Godhead. It is because we dwell in this realm that we enjoy God's protection, His day-to-day provision, all the blessings of His favor. But no one dwells there who still walks according to the course of this world, according to the prince of the power of the air, and under the control of the spirit that now works in the sons of disobedience. We are no longer "children of wrath" but "children of God" (John 1:12; 1 John 3:1) and citizens of heaven (Ephesians 2:19).

Just as in the old realm of sin and death we were subject to the prince of the power of the air (Ephesians 2:2), so in this new realm we follow a new Lord. Just as we were "by nature children of wrath" (v. 3) and "sons of disobedience" (v. 2), so now we are by nature "alive together with Christ" (v. 5) and "in Christ Jesus" (v. 6).

God's ultimate purpose in our salvation is to exalt His sovereign grace in order "that in the ages to come He might show the surpassing riches of His grace in kindness toward us in Christ Jesus" (v. 7 NASB). So our loving Father glorifies Himself even as He blesses us. His grace is the centerpiece of His glory. From the first moment of salvation throughout "the ages to come," we never stop benefiting from His grace and goodness to us. At no point does grace stop and human effort take over.

REDEEMED

I recently read a book written by a modern seminary professor who is very well known for his popular books on human relationships, psychology, religion, and related topics. His latest book deals with the subject of human shame. He began by recounting his saintly mother's death. As she lay dying she told him, "I'm so glad that the Lord forgives me all of my sins; I've been a great sinner, you know."

"Great sinner?" he wrote incredulously. "As far back as I can remember, she was on her knees scrubbing people's kitchen floors most days, up to her neck in the frets of five fussing children every evening, and, when late night fell, there she was on her knees again . . . asking the Lord for strength to do it again for one more day."[1]

His assessment was that his mother was inflicted with "a classic case of unhealthy shame." He wrote, "It saddens me still that such a triumph of a woman should have to die feeling like a wretch. Her shame was totally out of touch with her reality. She did not deserve to be stuck with so much shame."[2]

Yet the professor acknowledges that in both her living and her dying, his mother was "wondrously serene. She was given a grace to turn her shame into peace with a life tougher than she deserved."[3]

Evidently her statements about being a "great sinner" reflected nothing but the godly response of a chastened and transformed heart. Her lament was only an echo of what we all should feel when we realize the nature and the profound depth of our sinfulness (Romans 7:24). Why this man concluded his mother's shame was "unhealthy" and undeserved is not entirely clear.

After all, didn't even the apostle Paul describe himself as foremost of all sinners (1 Timothy 1:15)? Peter fell on his face before Christ and said, "Depart from me, for I am a sinful man, O Lord" (Luke 5:8). Isaiah, the most godly man in all Israel, said, "Woe is me, for I am ruined! Because I am a man of unclean lips, and I live among a people of unclean lips" (Isaiah 6:5 NASB). The greatest saints of history have all felt the same deep sense of shame.

But this professor suggests that we really are not so vile after all. In fact, he believes we are *worthy* of divine grace: "If grace heals all our shame, it must be a grace that tells us we are worthy to have it. We need, I believe, to recognize that we are accepted not only in spite of our undeserving but because of our worth."[4] He distinguishes between "deserving" and "worthy" like this: "If I deserve some good that comes my way, it is because I *did* something to earn it. If I am worthy, it is because I *am* somebody of enormous value."[5]

But does Scripture portray sinful humanity as inherently "worthy" of God's favor? Not at all. Nowhere in Scripture are we told we are "accepted because of our worth." Grace is *grace* precisely because it comes to people who are utterly ineligible for any favor from God: "While we were still *helpless* . . . Christ died for the ungodly. . . . While we were yet *sinners*, Christ died for us. . . . While we were *enemies* we were reconciled to God through the death of His Son" (Romans 5:6, 8, 10 NASB, emphasis added). Paul's very point in those verses is to suggest the supreme marvel of God's grace—that it should be extended to helpless, sinful, undeserving, even loathsome, adversaries.

Look, for example, at Daniel's prayer of repentance: "Righteousness belongs to You, O Lord, but to us *open shame*, as it is this day—to the men of Judah, the inhabitants of Jerusalem and all Israel, those who are nearby and those who are far away in all the countries to which You have driven them, because of their unfaithful deeds which they have committed against You. *Open shame belongs to us, O Lord, to our kings, our princes and our fathers, because we have sinned against You*" (Daniel 9:7–8 NASB, emphasis added).

Daniel would hardly have been an advocate of self-esteem theology!

The Bible simply does not speak of sinners as intrinsically worthy of God's grace. The prodigal son, Jesus' illustration of a repentant sinner, admitted his unworthiness (Luke 15:21). Even John the Baptist—who by Jesus' own testimony was the greatest prophet who ever lived (Matthew 11:11)—said he was *unworthy* to carry the shoes of the Savior (Matthew 3:11). "What is man that You are mindful of him, and the son of man that You visit him?" (Psalm 8:4). The reasons for God's grace to sinners are a mystery. We certainly are never told that God loves us because we are worthy. That notion is simply an echo of worldly self-esteem doctrine.

The focus of Scripture is entirely on *God's* worth, *His* majesty, *His* glory, *His* holiness, and *His* grace and mercy. Our worth as Christians is a *product* of God's grace, certainly not the *reason* for it. If people were inherently worthy of salvation, God would be unrighteous not to save everyone. But we are *saved* by grace—redeemed!

VICTORY

Because salvation is forever, our immortal souls are eternally beyond sin's reach. But sin *can* attack

Christians in their mortal bodies. Even our bodies will someday be glorified and forever be out of sin's reach, but as long as this life lasts we are subject to corruption and death. "This perishable must put on the imperishable, and this mortal must put on immortality" (1 Corinthians 15:53 NASB). Until then our mortal bodies are still subject to sin. That is why "we . . . groan within ourselves, waiting eagerly for our adoption as sons, the redemption of our body" (Romans 8:23 NASB).

Therefore Paul said, "Do not go on presenting the members of your body to sin as instruments of unrighteousness; but present yourselves to God as those alive from the dead, and your members as instruments of righteousness to God" (Romans 6:13 NASB). This parallels Romans 12:1: "I urge you therefore, brethren, by the mercies of God, to present your *bodies* a living and holy sacrifice, acceptable to God, which is your spiritual service of worship" (NASB, emphasis added), and "I discipline my *body* and make it my slave, so that, after I have preached to others, I myself will not be disqualified" (1 Corinthians 9:27 NASB, emphasis added).

Many interpreters have been tripped up by the verb tenses in Romans 6:12–13 (NASB). "Do not let sin reign" and "do not go on presenting" are present active imperative verbs. They are contrasted with an aorist imperative, "but present yourselves to God." At first glance it seems the apostle could be saying,

"*Stop* letting sin reign and *stop* yielding your members to sin, but submit yourselves to God," implying that these people were Christians who had never surrendered to Christ's lordship. But the context clearly indicates otherwise.

Paul also reminds them, "you became obedient from the heart" (Romans 6:17); "you became slaves of righteousness" (v. 18); and "[you were] freed from sin and enslaved to God" (v. 22 NASB). These are not people who have never surrendered. Here, and in Romans 12:1–2, Paul was simply encouraging them to keep surrendering in practice what they had already surrendered in principle. He was calling for decisive, deliberate surrender in their lives right now.

Is the outcome in doubt? Certainly not. In Romans 6:14, Paul offers these assuring words: "Sin shall not be master over you, for you are not under law but under grace" (NASB). The Christian is no longer under the condemning power of God's law but is now under the redeeming power of His grace. It is in the power of that grace, by faith, that the Lord now calls him to live.

ALL THINGS

Remember that when Paul wrote Romans, he was writing to first-century believers who would be terribly persecuted for their faith. Yet he could write, "All things work together for good to those who love God" (Romans 8:28). That's a verse memorized and regularly quoted by Christians, but imagine what it means to believers who have lost everything for the sake of Christ. Yet God's promise is sure; He continues to give us His grace.

God regularly and consistently takes all that He allows to happen to Christians, even what seems to them to be the worst things, and turns those events ultimately into blessings. That is divine providence at work.

No matter what your situation—happy, prosperous, and easy; or sad, painful, and difficult—through it all, God works to do what is ultimately best and most blessed for you.

In His providence, the Lord uses "all things," circumstances that are evil and harmful as well as those that are good and helpful, to mold you into the kind of person He wants you to be. When you struggle with life, just remember what God promised the apostle Paul, "My grace is sufficient for you, for My strength is made perfect in weakness" (2 Corinthians 12:9). That pledge is for you as well.

CHAPTER 5

GRACE LIVED OUT

Being recipients of such amazing grace, our lives need to show our gratitude to our Savior.

Paul wrote, "I press toward the goal for the prize of the upward call of God in Christ Jesus" (Philippians 3:14). The apostle Paul's goal was to be like Christ. He knew that he would receive his reward when God's upward call came. Like Paul, we won't reach the goal of Christlikeness in this life, but we will receive it instantly in the next: "It has not yet been revealed what we shall be, but we know that when He is revealed, we shall be like Him, for we shall see Him as He is" (1 John 3:2).

The upward call of God is our motivation to run the race. We should live in light of being called out of this world at any time into the presence of God, where we will receive our eternal reward. We were vile, godless sinners on our way to hell when God sovereignly chose us for salvation.

RUN THE RACE

Paul reminded the Corinthian believers, "Run in such a way that you may win" (1 Corinthians 9:24 NASB).

Because I was athletic as a boy, I played on many different teams in various sports programs. I remember many boys with little or no athletic ability who would try out for these teams. Every once in a while, a coach would feel sorry for such a boy and place him on the team in spite of his performance. He would give the boy a uniform to make him feel that he was a part of the team even though he would never let the boy play in a game.

We are all like the boy who had no ability. God graciously puts us on the team, not because of our own ability, but purely by His sovereign grace. And He gives us the ability to play the game. So get in the game and give thanks for the holy privilege of serving Jesus Christ.

FREEDOM

"But," you may be asking, "if grace is, by definition, 'free,' and our salvation is secure, wouldn't a person be tempted to then just live as he or she pleased?"

That way of thinking is called "antinomianism" ("against the law" or "no law"), and Paul counters it in Romans 6:

> What then? Shall we sin because we are not under
> law but under grace? May it never be! Do you not

know that when you present yourselves to someone as slaves for obedience, you are slaves of the one whom you obey, either of sin resulting in death, or of obedience resulting in righteousness? But thanks be to God that though you were slaves of sin, you became obedient from the heart to that form of teaching to which you were committed, and having been freed from sin, you became slaves of righteousness. (vv. 15–18 NASB)

Freedom from the law means freedom from sin's bondage and freedom from the law's penalty—not freedom from moral restraint. Grace does not mean we have permission to do as we please; it means we have the power to do what pleases God. The mere suggestion that God's grace gives us license to sin is self-contradictory, for the very purpose of grace is to free us from sin. How can we who are the recipients of grace continue in sin?

"May it never be!" is the same powerful and unequivocal denial Paul gave in Romans 6:2 (NASB). This truth needs no proof; it is self-evident: "Do you not know?" implies that *everyone* should understand something so basic. What could be more obvious? When you present yourselves to someone as slaves for obedience, you are slaves of the one whom you obey! There are only two choices. If our lives are characterized by sin, then we are sin's slaves. If we are characterized by obedience, then we are slaves of righteousness (vv. 16–18). Either way, we are not our own masters.

It is equally true that "no one can serve two masters; for either he will hate the one and love the other, or else he will be loyal to the one and despise the other. You cannot serve God and mammon" (Matthew 6:24). You cannot serve God and sin. Those who think they are Christians but are enslaved to sin are sadly deceived. We cannot have two contradictory natures at the same time. We cannot live in two opposing spiritual domains simultaneously. We cannot serve two masters. We are either slaves of sin by natural birth, or slaves of righteousness by regeneration. We can't be both in the Spirit and in the flesh (Romans 8:5–9).

Paul was not teaching the Romans that they *ought to be* slaves of righteousness. He was reminding them that they *are* slaves of righteousness. He told the Colossians the same thing: "Although you were formerly alienated and hostile in mind, engaged in evil deeds, yet He has now reconciled you in His fleshly body through death, in order to present you before Him holy and blameless and beyond reproach" (Colossians 1:21–22 NASB). For the Christian, the life of unrighteousness and hostility toward God is in the *past.* No true believer will continue indefinitely in disobedience, because sin is diametrically opposed to our new and holy nature. Real Christians cannot endure perpetually sinful living.

Paul thus reminded the Romans that they are no longer enslaved to sin: "Thanks be to God that though you were slaves of sin, you became obedient from the heart to that form of teaching to which you were committed" (Romans 6:17 NASB). Paul was not speaking about a legalistic or mechanical show of righteousness: "You became obedient from the heart." Grace transforms a person's innermost being. A person whose heart has not been changed is not saved. The hallmark of grace is an obedient heart.

Again, we must be clear: obedience does not produce or maintain salvation, but it is the inevitable characteristic of those who are saved. The desire to know and obey God's truth is one of the surest marks of genuine salvation. Jesus made it clear that those who obey His word are the true believers (John 8:31; 14:21, 23–24; 15:10).

Slaves of sin—unbelievers—are free from righteousness (Romans 6:20). Christians, on the other hand, are free from sin and enslaved to God through faith in Jesus Christ (v. 22). The inevitable benefit is sanctification, and the ultimate outcome is eternal life (v. 22). This promise sums up the whole point of Roman 6: God not only frees us from sin's penalty (justification), but He frees us from sin's tyranny as well (sanctification).

Nevertheless, though we are no longer subject to sin's dominion, all of us struggle desperately with sin in our lives.

CRUCIFIED WITH CHRIST

Paul wrote elsewhere, "I have been crucified with Christ; it is no longer I who live, but Christ lives in me" (Galatians 2:20). But in what sense are we dead to sin? All honest Christians will testify that we are still tempted, we still fall, we are still guilty of sin all the time. What did Paul mean by saying believers have "died to sin"?

He is talking about our union with Christ. All believers are joined to Christ by faith:

> Do you not know that all of us who have been baptized into Christ Jesus have been baptized into His death? Therefore we have been buried with Him through baptism into death, so that as Christ was raised from the dead through the glory of the Father, so we too might walk in newness of life. For if we have become united with Him in the likeness of His death, certainly we shall be also in the likeness of His resurrection. (Romans 6:3–5)

The phrase "baptized into Christ Jesus . . . baptized into His death" has nothing to do with water baptism. Paul was using the expression *baptizo-* in the same way he employed it in 1 Corinthians 10:2, where he spoke of the Israelites as having been "baptized into Moses." *Baptized into* in that sense means "identified with," "linked to." In Galatians 3:27, Paul said, "All of you who were baptized into Christ have clothed yourselves with Christ" (NASB). Again, he was speaking of *union with Christ*: "The one who joins himself to the Lord is one spirit with Him" (1 Corinthians 6:17 NASB).

Our union with Christ is the premise on which justification, sanctification, and every other aspect of God's saving work hinge. If we would understand our salvation, we must first grasp what it means to be united with Christ. About this doctrine, Martyn Lloyd-Jones wrote,

> We are actually in union with Christ and to him. You cannot have read the New Testament even cursorily without noticing this constantly repeated phrase—"in Christ"—"in Christ Jesus." The apostles go on repeating it and it is one of the most significant and glorious statements in the entire realm and range of truth. It means that we are joined to the Lord Jesus Christ; we have become a part of him. We are in him. We belong

to him. We are members of his body. And the teaching is that God regards us as such; and this, of course, means that now, *in this relationship, we are sharers in, and partakers of, everything that is true of the Lord Jesus Christ himself.*[1]

"As in Adam all die, even so in Christ all shall be made alive" (1 Corinthians 15:22). "In Adam" describes the state of the unregenerate person still in bondage to sin, dying, unable to please God in any way. But "in Christ" describes precisely the opposite state, the position of every true believer in Christ. We are free from sin's tyranny, able to love and obey God from the heart, partakers in all the blessedness of Christ Himself, the objects of God's loving favor, destined for a glorious eternity. "There is therefore now no condemnation for those who are in Christ Jesus" (Romans 8:1).

Our union with Christ results in some very dramatic changes. First of all, we are justified. Justification takes place in the court of God. It is a divine "not guilty" verdict. The term *justification* does not describe the actual change in the sinner's character; it describes the change in his or her standing before God.

But because we are united with Christ, changes in our very nature occur as well. *Regeneration, conversion,* and *sanctification* are the words that describe that change. We are born again—*regenerated*—given a new heart, a new spirit, and a new love for God

(Ezekiel 36:26; 1 John 4:19–20). We become partakers of the divine nature (2 Peter 1:3–4). We are raised to walk in newness of life (Romans 6:4). And the old sinful self is put to death: "Knowing this, that our old self was crucified with Him, in order that our body of sin might be done away with, so that we should no longer be slaves to sin; for he who has died is freed from sin" (Romans 6:6–7 NASB).

We should deal with our sin courageously, striking at its head. Subduing it a little bit is not enough. We need to exterminate it, hack it in pieces—seek by the means of grace and the power of the Spirit to wring the deadly life from it.

It is a lifelong task, in which our progress will always be only gradual. That may make the fight seem daunting at first. But as soon as we set ourselves to the work, we discover that sin shall *not* be master over us, for we are under grace (Romans 6:14). That means it is God who is at work in us both to will and to work for His good pleasure (Philippians 2:13). And having begun His good work in us, He "will perfect it until the day of Christ Jesus" (Philippians 1:6 NASB).

Paul inserts a glorious promise at this point: "Sin shall not be master over you, for you are not under law, but under grace" (Romans 6:14 NASB). We are free from sin's condemnation because of our justification. But grace also frees us from sin's day-to-day domination, so that we can become "slaves of righteousness" (Romans 6:18)—so that we can obey a new Lord.

OBEDIENCE

The very purpose of grace is to free us from sin—"so we too might walk in newness of life" (Romans 6:4 NASB). Grace is much more than mere forgiveness for our sins, or a free ride to heaven. Grace certainly does not leave us under sin's dominion. Saved by grace, "we are [God's own] workmanship, created in Christ Jesus for good works, which God prepared beforehand that we should walk in them" (Ephesians 2:10). Grace "[instructs] us to deny ungodliness and worldly desires and to live sensibly, righteously and godly in the present age" (Titus 2:12 NASB). This is the very reason Christ gave Himself for us: "That He might redeem us from every lawless deed and purify for Himself a people for His own possession, zealous for good deeds" (Titus 2:14 NASB).

Yet it seems there have always been those who have corrupted the grace of God by turning it into lasciviousness (Jude v. 4). They characterize grace as total freedom, but they themselves are enslaved to corruption (2 Peter 2:19). Thus they nullify the grace of God (Galatians 2:21).

"The true grace of God" (1 Peter 5:12) does not offer freedom from moral restraint. Grace is no sanction for sin. On the contrary, it grants the believer freedom *from* sin. It frees us from the law and from sin's penalty, but it also liberates us from sin's absolute control. It frees us to obey God.

Anticipating the thoughts of those who misunderstand God's grace, Paul echoed his query from Romans 6:1: "What then? Shall we sin because we are not under law but under grace?" (Romans 6:15). And he answers once again emphatically, "May it never be!"

His argument against the objection is an appeal to common sense: "Do you not know that when you present yourselves to someone as slaves for obedience, you are slaves of the one whom you obey, either of sin resulting in death, or of obedience resulting in righteousness?" (Romans 6:16 NASB). In other words, if you present yourself as a slave to do sin's bidding, you only demonstrate that you are still under sin's dominion. The clear implication is that those truly saved by grace would not willingly choose to return to the old slavery.

In fact, the phrase "present yourselves" suggests a conscious, active, willing *choice* of obedience. It pictures a soldier who presents himself with all his weapons to his commander, prepared to do the master's bidding. It is a voluntary, deliberate surrender of oneself and one's members to a life of service—either to "sin resulting in death, or [to] obedience resulting in righteousness." Here Paul is calling for a deliberate, willful, conscious choice of obedience. For unbelievers, there is no choice. They are enslaved to sin and cannot choose otherwise. Here Paul is suggesting that genuine Christians also have only one choice.

In other words, those who choose to serve sin as its slaves are in fact still enslaved to sin—they have never experienced God's grace. "When you present yourselves to someone as slaves for obedience, you are slaves of the one whom you obey." That at first may sound like a tautology, but a paraphrase may help explain the apostle's meaning: "When you voluntarily relinquish yourself to sin and its service, you give evidence that you were never freed from sin's dominion to begin with. Your pattern of life proves who your true master is—whether sin unto death, or obedience that results in righteousness." Or, as Peter wrote, "By what a man is overcome, by this he is enslaved" (2 Peter 2:19 NASB).

In Romans 5, Paul makes precisely the same point, only arguing in reverse. There he suggests that sin and death reign over all those in Adam (v. 12); but grace, righteousness, and eternal life reign over the one who is in Christ (vv. 17–20).

In Romans 6, Paul suggests that everyone is a slave who has a master. Fallen man likes to declare that he is the master of his fate and the captain of his soul. But no one really is. All people are either under Satan's lordship and in bondage to sin, or they are under Christ's lordship and servants of righteousness. There is no neutral ground, and no one can serve two masters (Matthew 6:24). "If we would know to which of these two families we belong, we must inquire to which of these two masters we yield our obedience."[2] *Paul's point was that true Christians cannot be anything but slaves of righteousness.*

Again, Paul was not telling the Romans that Christians *ought to be* slaves of righteousness. His point was that true Christians *cannot be anything but* slaves of righteousness. They were taken out of sin's servitude for precisely that purpose: "Thanks be to God that though you were slaves of sin, you became obedient from the heart to that form of teaching to which you were committed, and having been freed from sin, you became slaves of righteousness" (Romans 6:17–18 NASB).

That corresponds exactly to what the apostle John wrote: "No one who is born of God practices sin, because His seed abides in him; and he cannot sin, because he is born of God. By this the children of God and the children of the devil are obvious: anyone who does not practice righteousness is not of God" (1 John 3:9–10 NASB).

For the Christian, the life of slavery to sin is *past*. Sin cannot continue to be the chief characteristic of our lives. Fleshly disobedience interrupts the new life frequently and we do sin. At times sin may *appear* to dominate a Christian's life completely (as was the case when David sinned). But all true believers still have a new and holy nature. They hate their sin and love righteousness. They cannot live in unbroken sin or hardened rebellion against God and enjoy it. That would be a contradiction of who they are (1 John 3:9).

GOOD WORKS

"So, since we have this freedom and are no longer slaves to sin, what's the connection between our faith for salvation and our good works?" you may ask.

Those who believe that it is possible to claim Christ as Savior but not as Lord—"no-lordship theology"— would say there is no direct connection. Immediately following Ephesians 2:8–9 (the great affirmation of being saved "by grace . . . through faith"), however, Paul adds verse 10: "We are His workmanship, created in Christ Jesus for good works, which God prepared beforehand that we should walk in them." That is a verse no-lordship theology cannot adequately explain. Many no-lordship books have simply ignored it. Verses 8 and 9 may seem to fit easily into the no-lordship system. But without verse 10 we do not have the full picture of what Paul was saying about our salvation.

It cannot be overemphasized that works play no role in gaining salvation. But good works have everything to do with living out salvation. No good works can earn salvation, but many good works result from genuine salvation. Good works are not necessary to become a disciple, but good works are the necessary marks of all true disciples. God has, after all, ordained that we should walk in them.

Note that before we can do any good work for the Lord, He does His good work in us. By God's grace we become "His workmanship, created in Christ Jesus for good works." The same grace that made us alive with Christ and raised us up with Him enables us to do the good works unto which He has saved us. Note also that it is God who "prepared" these good works. We get no credit for them. Even our good works are works of His grace. It would also be appropriate to call them "grace works." They are the corroborating evidence of true salvation. These works, like every other aspect of divine salvation, are the product of God's sovereign grace.

Good deeds and righteous attitudes are intrinsic to who we are as Christians. They proceed from the very nature of one who lives in the realm of the heavenlies. Just as the unsaved are sinners by nature, the redeemed are righteous by nature. Paul told the Corinthians that God's abundant grace provided an overflowing sufficiency that equipped them "for every good work" (2 Corinthians 9:8). He told Titus that

Christ "gave Himself for us, that He might redeem us from every lawless deed and purify for Himself His own special people, zealous for good works" (Titus 2:14).

Remember that Paul's primary message here is not evangelistic. He is writing to believers, many of whom had come to Christ years earlier. His point is not to tell them how to be saved, but to remind them of how they were saved, so that they could see how grace is meant to operate in the lives of the redeemed. The phrase "we are His workmanship" is the key to this whole passage.

The Greek word for workmanship is *poiema*, from which we get poem. Our lives are like a divinely written sonnet, a literary masterpiece. From eternity past, God designed us to be conformed to the image of His Son (Romans 8:29). All of us are still imperfect, unfinished works of art being carefully crafted by the divine Master. He is not finished with us yet, and His work will not cease until He has made us into the perfect likeness of His Son (1 John 3:2).

The energy He uses to accomplish His work is grace. Sometimes the process is slow and arduous; sometimes it is immediately triumphant. Either way, "I am confident of this very thing, that He who began a good work in you will perfect it until the day of Christ Jesus" (Philippians 1:6 NASB).

Cheap grace? No way. Nothing about true grace is cheap. It cost God His Son. Its value is inestimable.

Its effects are eternal. But it is free—"freely bestowed on us in the Beloved" (Ephesians 1:6 NASB)—and it "abound[s] to many" (Romans 5:15), elevating us into that heavenly realm where God has ordained that we should walk.

LAW VERSUS GRACE

Still, the harsh reality is that every Christian fails to follow Christ perfectly, because every Christian has a sinful nature. Yet there's an important distinction between legal obedience and gracious obedience.

Legal obedience is the result of fleshly effort. It demands an absolute, perfect obedience without a single failure. It says that if you violate God's law even once, the penalty is death.

Gracious obedience is a loving and sincere spirit of submission motivated by God's grace to us. Though often defective, this obedience is nevertheless accepted by God, for its blemishes are blotted out by the blood of Jesus Christ.

What a difference! With fleshly, human effort, obedience must be perfect to be of any value. With divine grace, God looks at the heart, not the works. If God measured my legal obedience against His standard, I would spend eternity in hell. But God looks at me and sees a heart redeemed by Christ that longs to obey Him and a spirit that wills to submit to His lordship, even though that willingness is far from perfect.

Do you remember when Peter was frustrated in convincing the Lord that he, though disobedient, loved Him? What did Peter finally say to get the Lord to accept his confession of love? He didn't say, "Look at my obedience," since he was caught disobeying. He said, "Lord, You know all things; You know that I love You" (John 21:17). That is the point of the cross of Christ. Jesus died, bearing the full penalty for our sins and failings, so that His blood can cover whatever is defective in our day-to-day love and obedience.

Certainly even the apostles didn't always obey God. All of them failed the Lord and made mistakes because they, too, were sinful. Yet concerning them, Jesus could tell the Father, "They have kept Your word" (John 17:6). Did they keep it perfectly? Of course not. Their desire and determination to submit to Jesus Christ were what Jesus measured, not a legalistic, absolute standard.

God's standard of holiness is still absolute perfection, but He has graciously made provision for our inevitable failures. If we do something wrong, He doesn't say we are no longer Christians. He looks with favor on those who have a spirit of obedience. The true Christian has a desire to submit to Jesus Christ, even though he can't always fulfill that desire. But God discerns and graciously accepts it.

God knows what's inside because He has written His law in your heart: "I will put My law in their minds, and write it on their hearts; and I will be their God, and they shall be My people" (Jeremiah 31:33). Psalm 40:8 says, "I delight to do Your will, O my God, and Your law is within my heart." Scripture confirms that whatever is in a man's heart controls how he lives: "For as he thinks in his heart, so is he" (Proverbs 23:7). Those who truly know God—those who love Him—will be moved in their hearts to obey the law God wrote there.

LIVING LIKE JESUS

Early in His ministry, Jesus told the disciples what He expected of them, of all His true followers, in what is called "the Sermon on the Mount."

Jesus' sermon begins with the beatitudes—that familiar series of blessings on the poor in spirit, pure in heart, peacemakers, and persecuted. There are eight beatitudes in Matthew's account, and combined, they describe the true nature of saving faith.

- Blessed are the poor in spirit, for theirs is the kingdom of heaven.
- Blessed are those who mourn, for they shall be comforted.

- Blessed are the meek, for they shall inherit the earth.
- Blessed are those who hunger and thirst for righteousness, for they shall be filled.
- Blessed are the merciful, for they shall obtain mercy.
- Blessed are the pure in heart, for they shall see God.
- Blessed are the peacemakers, for they shall be called sons of God.
- Blessed are those who are persecuted for righteousness' sake, for theirs is the kingdom of heaven.
- Blessed are you when they revile and persecute you, and say all kinds of evil against you falsely for My sake.
- Rejoice and be exceedingly glad, for great is your reward in heaven, for so they persecuted the prophets who were before you. (Matthew 5:3–12)

The "poor in spirit" (v. 3) are those who know they have no spiritual resources of their own. "Those who mourn" (v. 4) are repentant people, truly sorrowful over their own sin. "The meek" (v. 5) are those who truly fear God and know their own unworthiness in light of His holiness. "Those who hunger and thirst for righteousness" (v. 6) are those who, having turned from sin, yearn for what God loves instead. Those four beatitudes are all *inward qualities* of authentic faith. They describe the believer's state of heart. More specifically, they describe how the believer sees himself before God: poor, sorrowful, meek, and hungry.

The final four beatitudes describe the *outward manifestations* of those qualities. They focus mainly on the believer's moral character, and they describe what the authentic Christian should look like to an objective observer. "The merciful" (v. 7) are those who, as beneficiaries of God's grace, extend grace to others. "The pure in heart" (v. 8) describes people whose thoughts and actions are characterized by holiness. "The peacemakers" (v. 9) speaks mainly of those who spread the message of "peace with God through our Lord Jesus Christ" (Romans 5:1)—which is the only true and lasting peace. And obviously, "those who are persecuted for righteousness' sake" (Matthew 5:10) are citizens of Christ's kingdom who suffer because of their affiliation with Him and their faithfulness to Him. The world hates them because it hates Him (John 15:18; 1 John 3:1, 13).

The order is significant. The more faithfully a person lives out the first seven beatitudes, the more he or she will experience the persecution spoken of in the eighth.

All those qualities are radically at odds with the world's values. The world esteems pride more than humility; loves merriment rather than mourning; thinks strong-willed assertiveness is superior to true meekness; and prefers the satiety of carnal pleasure over a thirst for real righteousness. The world looks with utter contempt on holiness and purity of heart, scorns every plea to make peace with God, and constantly persecutes the truly righteous. Jesus could hardly have devised a list of virtues more at odds with His culture.

SUMMARY OF GRACE

We have defined grace as "the free and benevolent influence of a holy God operating sovereignly in the lives of undeserving sinners."

True grace is more than just a giant freebie, opening the door to heaven in the sweet by and by, but leaving us to wallow in sin in the bitter here and now. Grace is God presently at work in our lives. By grace "we are His workmanship, created in Christ Jesus for good works, which God prepared beforehand, that we should walk in them" (Ephesians 2:10). By grace He "gave Himself for us, that He might redeem us from every lawless deed and purify for Himself a people for His own possession, zealous for good deeds" (Titus 2:14).

That ongoing work of grace in the Christian's life is as much a certainty as justification, glorification, or any other aspect of God's redeeming work. "I am confident of this very thing, that He who began a good work in you will perfect it until the day of Christ Jesus" (Philippians 1:6 NASB). Salvation is wholly God's work, and He finishes what He starts. His grace *is* sufficient. And potent. It cannot be defective in any regard. "Grace" that does not affect one's behavior is not the grace of God.

NOTES

Chapter 1: Grace Defined

1. A. W. Tozer, *The Knowledge of the Holy* (New York: Harper & Row, 1961), 100.
2. Louis Berkhof, *Systematic Theology* (Grand Rapids, MI: Eerdmans, 1939), 427.
3. Ibid.
4. This is contrary to Zane Hodges' staggering claim, "It is inherently contradictory to speak here of 'grace' as the 'gift of God.' The *giving of a gift is an act* of 'grace,' but 'grace,' when viewed as a principle or basis of divine action, is never said to be a 'gift,' or part of a gift" (*Absolutely Free!* [Grand Rapids, MI: Zondervan, 1989], 219). Scripture is filled with statements that contradict that assertion: "The Lord gives grace and glory; no good thing does He withhold from those who walk uprightly" (Ps. 84:11); "He gives grace to the afflicted"

(Prov. 3:34); "He gives a greater grace" (James 4:6); "God is opposed to the proud, but gives grace to the humble" (1 Peter 5:5; also Rom. 15:15; 1 Cor. 1:4; 3:10; Eph. 4:7).

5. Charles Ryrie, *So Great Salvation* (Wheaton, IL: Victor, 1989), 18.

6. Ibid., 142.

7. Zane Hodges, *Absolutely Free!* (Grand Rapids, MI: Zondervan, 1989), 73–74.

Chapter 4: Grace Realized

1. Lewis B. Smedes, *Shame and Grace: Healing the Shame We Don't Deserve* (San Francisco: HarperCollins, 1993), 3–4.

2. Ibid., 4.

3. Ibid.

4. Ibid., 119.

5. Ibid., 120.

Chapter 5: Grace Lived Out

1. D. Martyn Lloyd-Jones, *Sanctified Through the Truth: The Assurance of Our Salvation* (Wheaton: Crossway, 1989), 116–17, emphasis added.

2. Matthew Henry, *Commentary on the Whole Bible*, 6 vols. (Old Tappan, NJ: Revell, n.d.], 6:405.

ABOUT THE AUTHOR

Widely known for his thorough, candid approach to teaching God's Word, John MacArthur is a popular author and conference speaker and has served as pastor-teacher of Grace Community Church in Sun Valley, California, since 1969. John and his wife, Patricia, have four grown children and fifteen grandchildren.

John's pulpit ministry has been extended around the globe through his media ministry, Grace to You, and its satellite offices in seven countries. In addition to producing daily radio programs for nearly 2,000 English and Spanish radio outlets worldwide, Grace to You distributes books, software, audiotapes, and CDs by John MacArthur.

John is president of The Master's College and Seminary and has written hundreds of books and study guides, each one biblical and practical. Best-selling titles include *The Gospel According to Jesus, The Truth War, The Murder of Jesus, Twelve Ordinary Men,*

Twelve Extraordinary Women, and *The MacArthur Study Bible,* a 1998 ECPA Gold Medallion recipient.

For more details about John MacArthur and his Bible-teaching resources, contact Grace to You at 800-55-GRACE or www.gty.org.

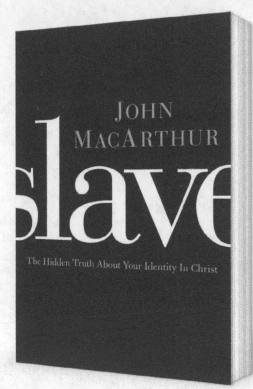

THE TRUTH ABOUT SERIES

THE TRUTH ABOUT . . . Grace

THE TRUTH ABOUT . . . The Lordship
of Christ

THE TRUTH ABOUT . . . Forgiveness

Available wherever books and ebooks are sold.

THOMAS NELSON
Since 1798

Printed in the USA
CPSIA information can be obtained
at www.ICGtesting.com
LVHW051536210724
785408LV00010B/169